GOODBYE, MUMMY

To Jim
With Love
Best Wishes
From
Sickue

Susan

16·10·11
x

GOODBYE, MUMMY DARLING

by

SUSAN TICKNER

**MORAN
PUBLICATIONS**

© Susan Tickner 2003
First published in 2003 by Moran Publications
Reprinted in 2004
1 Courville Close, Alveston
Bristol BS35 3RR

The right of Susan Tickner to be identified as the author of
the work has been asserted herein in accordance with the
Copyright, Designs and Patents Act 1988.

British Library Cataloguing in Publication Data
A catalogue record for this book is available from the British
Library

ISBN 0-9541290-0-8

Typeset by Amolibros, Milverton, Somerset
This book production has been managed by Amolibros
Printed and bound by Advance Book Printing, Oxford, UK

In memory of

Sean, Flo

& Denise

who are always there for us.

The inspiration for writing this book came from my daughter Wendy, and my three sons, Paul, Sean and Denis. Without their true love and understanding and our togetherness as a family, this true story would not have been written.

May time never run out for those still waiting to be united with their loved ones.

ACKNOWLEDGEMENTS

It is always difficult to give thanks to those who help you in time of need primarily in case you leave someone out and offend them. I have been offered and given so much help in compiling this story but there are some thank you's I have to put to paper. To everyone who has not been mentioned, and I am sure they know who they are, I apologise for not naming you.

At the top of the list come my children whose response to my needs over all their years epitomise what a family is all about.

To my loving husband for his patience, understanding and his often welcomed input.

Thanks also to my step brother and sisters who have through thick and thin embraced me as a full member of the family.

Particular thanks to my dear brother Roy who has suffered untold mental and emotional anguish for so long. Always my rock throughout my younger years I pray often for his happiness and peace of mind which, because of circumstances, can never be complete.

To my first and favourite employers the Annesley Motor Company, Dublin. Thank you for your support through my difficult times. It has been nice to maintain my links with you to the present day.

A mention too for my now dear friend, Vanya, who I met recently for the first time in forty-seven years. Vanya helped to fill in some gaps from past times in our shared childhood in

Australia together with the Drs Philip and, now sadly passed away, Phyllis Goatcher.

In the research of my early life I must single out Ian Thwaites of the Child Migrants Trust, Nottingham, whose quiet calming words stood me in good stead as I confronted ghosts of those unhappy times.

I must thank also Dursley (Gloucestershire) County Council for allowing me quick access to their archives in my search for the truth.

Finally, I take this opportunity to make reference to all those migrant children, everywhere. So many suffered and will never know real love or the bosom of a family. Many couldn't face life so, sadly, were driven to commit the cardinal sin. Some live on never knowing but always asking, why? I count myself so fortunate to have come through relatively unscathed but my heart goes out to those who didn't or never will.

ABOUT
THE AUTHOR

Susan Tickner was born in Cheltenham. At the age of three she was fostered out to several institutions in the UK. Then finally at the age of nine, she was sent to Australia as a child migrant.

Writing her life story *Goodbye, Mummy Darling* has given Susan the therapy she needed, and although sadness has dominated her life, bitterness does not. Her four children will always be her rock.

Since the recent death of her beloved husband, Susan spends most of her spare time writing poetry and walking her Jack Russell dogs, Holly and Jessie.

CHAPTER ONE

At a guess I'd say it must have been raining the day I was born because with most of us rain seems to conjure up a picture of misery, an appropriate omen for me coming into the world. It was Friday, 13th December 1943, and I was born to a mother who was French Canadian, the child of an unmarried mother. She had been put up for adoption in a Canadian orphanage and at the age of nine was adopted by an English couple and brought to England. My father was, I believe, of Scottish descent, although he was born in Singapore and his mother, my grandmother, died whilst giving birth to my father. He came to England and somehow, some twenty years later, both he and my mother met each other, married and had two sons, Alan and Roy, and then (on that supposedly rainy day!) me, Susan. This is my story going back to my earliest memories.

I was seven years old and my mother remarried when I was aged two so the family situation soon changed. My eldest brother, Alan, had gone to live with my father, while Roy and I now had a stepfather and a new addition to the family, a stepbrother, Rodney. I had developed into a very frightened child and my stepfather was so horrible to Roy and I that we felt like intruders in his new life. He did everything possible to make our lives miserable and punished us with beatings and abuse whenever he saw fit. My mother seemed to hide herself from all this behind her new family. Rodney was now one year old and my mother was heavily pregnant, so most of her time was taken up with other responsibilities.

I remember many childhood incidents and most of them bring back awful memories. On one occasion Roy and I were going to Sunday School, dressed accordingly, and were putting on our nicely polished shoes. My stepfather had a mania for polished shoes, having been in the army for many years and, because of this, every shoe in the house had to be polished every night before bedtime. He would inspect them and if he couldn't see his face in them we would get a clout around the head and be made to keep polishing until he could. We were, one morning, waiting for parental inspection, stood like two tin soldiers. 'Go on,' he shouted. 'Off you go and God help you if you get those shoes dirty,' and we would then run out of the door with a sense of freedom much like two young birds let out of a cage. We would skip up the street, holding hands, and Roy always took care of me because he knew that I was easily frightened, though sometimes he would play tricks on me and make me more frightened. Then I would cry and he would put his arm around me and say, 'Oh, come on, I didn't mean it.' I always felt safe with him and he was the only person in the whole world whom I really cared for. When I fell over and grazed my knees he was there to smooth them even though he would sometimes be angry and say, 'Don't be a baby.' But underneath all his bravado I knew he loved me.

He was so brave, much braver than me, and on this particular Sunday morning when we had set off for Sunday School he said to me, 'Don't let's go to Sunday School, the fair is on at the park; let's go there.'

'We can't,' I replied. 'Our dad will kill us.'

'Oh don't be a scaredy cat,' he retorted and with a sudden pull on my arm he yanked me in the direction of the park. We had a wonderful time. Roy always liked the dodgem cars, and I loved to watch the roundabout go round and round with the horses going up and down. We didn't have any money for rides, of course, but just to watch was more than enough for me and there was so much to see. Roy was busy hanging around the dodgem cars, waiting to see if he could get a free go. He would get on and when the man came around for the money I would watch him shout at Roy and make him get off. Yet sometimes, but not very often, he would seem to notice Roy but ignore him and let him have a free ride. I was too scared and stood at the railings just watching while he waved to me as he went around and around. We were of course children and like most children we didn't seem to take any notice of the time; we weren't even sure how long Sunday School lasted and what time we would be expected to arrive back home.

Another yank on the arm and Roy was saying, 'Come on, he'll kill us, we are miles late!' and I started to cry and he said, 'Oh, shut up, not now, come on, run!'

We ran all the way home, then hurried through the front gate, up the side path and through the back door. It must have looked like we had just fallen down a laundry chute and, still holding hands, frozen to the spot, we were greeted by our stepfather.

'Where have you been?' he roared, his eyes on me as I stood rigidly still, mouth agape, and said in a terrified squeaky voice:

'Sunday School, Dad.'

His eyes then turned to Roy: 'And you?' he asked.

'Up the fair, Dad,' Roy replied.

By this time Roy had let go of my hand; I felt completely alone, and I wanted to die. Even at that young age, I really wanted to die. Even before I could look at Roy and even try to ask him why he had done this to me, my stepfather had grabbed hold of me and was swinging me around, beating me, saying over and over how he would cure me of telling lies. I can remember my mother coming into the kitchen, pleading with him to put me down and leave me alone. He told her to get about her business and leave him to deal with me, swearing that he would teach me even if it was the last thing he ever did. He then put me down and told me to go to bed and stay there all day without any tea, and that the devil would probably come and take me away on the end of his pitch fork because that's what the devil did with liars.

I remember going to my room and throwing myself into bed and putting the sheet over my face and I could hear myself breathing and, for as long as I could, I held my breath in case the devil heard me and came and got me. I can't remember crying; I was too scared to cry, too scared to make any noise, and I lay very still in my bed until eventually exhaustion made me fall asleep. Sometimes, on this and similar occasions, my mother would sneak upstairs with a piece of cake or bread and butter and say a few gentle words to me but all the time I could see that she was too frightened herself, and would only stay for a very short time.

Roy had missed a beating this time because he had told the truth but he had been made to polish both his and my shoes until they were like a mirror. I lay in bed and could hear my stepfather yelling at him and telling him how lucky he was this time and that if he ever did anything like this again he would kill him.

There were so many times like this for Roy and me that it almost became the norm. It was the only way of life that we knew and assumed that it was the same for everyone and the reason that our stepbrother Rodney was treated differently was because he was only a baby. I have spent my entire life wondering why grown men sexually abuse young children. The horrid memories I have of my stepfather physically and mentally abusing me when I was a small child, and the torment of asking myself why my mother allowed this to happen continues to haunt me, to this day.

Roy and I stayed friends because I always forgave him. I didn't feel safe without him, and although he continued to play tricks on me and get me into trouble I adored him.

Soon, my mother had three young children—Rodney, Yvonne and Shirley, all the offspring of my stepfather. Shirley was still a small baby and slept in my parents' bedroom but Rodney and Yvonne were in with me. Because my stepfather didn't get up and go to work on a Sunday, the children would go into his bedroom and romp about and have fun. Roy and I were always

4

invited to join in this activity, which we did, but it wasn't always 'fun' for us as we knew that the invitation only came from our mother and that our stepfather would watch and wait for us to make one wrong move and do something wrong, so that we would be sent straight back to our beds. We loved our brothers and sisters and, although they seemed to get all the good attention, we didn't seem to mind this; it only seemed to bring us closer together.

One Sunday morning they all clambered out of bed into our parents' room, but I just lay there. I heard the others calling me but somehow felt that I couldn't move. I decided to go to the bathroom and went to get out of bed but I fell to the floor. I had no use in my legs and was too scared to say anything in case I got a hiding. I dragged myself to the bathroom on my stomach and then managed to get back into bed. Shortly afterwards my mother came to see where I was or perhaps more so, what I was up to. She asked what was wrong and I said I couldn't walk, that I couldn't feel my legs. She took off in a hurry back to her bedroom and after what only seemed to be a few minutes my stepfather was hurrying the others downstairs and telling them to stay in the back room. He then came upstairs to see me. I can remember always cowering when he came towards me I was so frightened of him. He asked what was wrong with me and threatened, 'If you're pretending, my girl, you'll know what for.'

I answered, 'I can't walk, Dad.' He pulled the bedclothes back then lifted me out of bed, and carried me downstairs into the front room which made me feel more scared because no one ever used the front room, except for Christmas and special occasions. He tried to put me down on the floor and I remember nearly falling to the ground. He told my mother to get the doctor and he laid me across the settee, put a cover over me and told me he would be back later when the doctor came.

I felt cold and alone and I asked my mother if the others could come in and I could watch them play. I could hear them in the other room all playing and I felt that nobody wanted me, that nobody had even noticed that I was missing. After what

5

seemed to be forever and a day the doctor arrived and after an examination there was much mumbling going on with my parents.

'Give her plenty of milk to drink,' said the doctor, 'while I call an ambulance and keep the others away from her. I suspect it's polio.' I didn't know what polio was but my parents seemed to because they began to panic and to sort of stand clear of me like I had the plague or something. I didn't know then, but that's exactly what polio was. I went off to hospital in the ambulance and somehow it all seemed great to me because I wasn't in any pain and I was getting all this attention. I felt rather special but after arriving at the hospital things got worse and I was put into an isolation ward and I was told that polio was very contagious and although they were not entirely sure that I had polio it was better to be safe than sorry.

This ward, just a small room, was very lonely, and hours and hours would go by without my seeing anybody. The nurse would come in the mornings to wash me and sit me up and she would ask me if I would like to try walking, and I would say no, I couldn't. Then, she would leave and someone would bring my meals and day by day the routine was the same. I had no visitors because I was still 'a risk to others' the staff would say. Days turned into weeks and weeks turned into months and, after seven months, I remember a doctor sitting on the side of my bed talking to me saying that he was completely baffled by my case and that he was going to try and see if he could get me to walk. He sat me up, and swung my legs out over the bed and attempted to get me to stand on the floor holding on to him and the bed. I got very upset, and started to cry and said, 'I can't, I can't!' so he put me back into bed. Several days after that, I woke one morning and without any thought at all I got out of bed and was standing by it when the nurse came in to wash me. She screamed ran out of the room and within moments was back with another nurse saying to her, 'Look, she's walking!'

The hospital became very busy that morning. Doctors came in and examined me and were completely puzzled and said that it must have been rheumatics. After that diagnosis they requested that I be moved to an open ward, which I was, and two weeks later I was sent back home. I have since learnt that my illness was trauma as a result of my stepfather's sexual abuse of me.

I remember being treated like a broken doll for the first few days but it didn't take long before things got back to normal and once again I was the outcast I had always been. In fact, things had got worse: I hadn't been missed, and now I was back in the way again and I heard my parents continually arguing.

'I don't want them here,' he would say, and my mother would reply, 'But they are my children, I can't just give them away.' My stepfather was the dominant one and what he said went, so before long they were making arrangements to send us away to a children's home. He now had three children of his own and he didn't want us mixing with them—'giving them bad habits' he would say. He didn't want us at all. All he wanted was for us to be out of the way for good so that he and my mother and Rodney, Yvonne and Shirley could have a nice cosy life. Nothing had changed; he had never wanted us in the first place and I remember my mother again pleading with him, 'Please don't send them away,' but he would ignore her or shout at her, always pointing out the fact that she was there to look after 'his' three children.

We later found ourselves, Roy and I, in a council care home for children although I have very little memory of this. Roy remained in the home and I was fostered out to a bank manager and his wife who lived in a place called Wootton Under Edge. I very soon found out that this was to be a living nightmare. Mr Bank Manager was very nice, but Mrs Bank Manager was dreadful. She would grab my hair and bang my head against the wall and say, 'You will call me Mother.' I was terrified of her. Whenever I asked for Roy, my brother, or my mother, she would say, 'They are gone now, I am your new mother.' Then I would rebel and struggle to get away from her but she was bigger and stronger than me and if I didn't 'behave', as she would put it, she would lock me in my room. When her husband came home from work he would sometimes find her bullying me and he would lock her in the attic until she calmed down, and, in a temper, she would bowl apples down the stairs, apples that had previously been put there to ripen off. I hated her and when she had been locked in the attic he would read me a story but I never felt happy. I wanted to be with Roy, my brother, because he was the only person that I had ever felt happy with. I am not sure how long I stayed with these people but once again I found myself back in the children's home. I remember something about this bank manager and his wife applying to adopt me but they were turned down for some reason.

The next memory I have is Roy and I sailing off from Tilbury Docks to Australia. I don't know how this happened, I have yet to find out, but I will: I am determined.

We both found ourselves with a group of children on board a ship named the SS *Chitral* which was set to sail from Tilbury Docks, London to Fremantle, Perth, Western Australia. I was nine years old and Roy was ten and a half, the other children in the group being all different ages from sixteen down to two years of age. I don't remember much of the outward journey, I don't remember even saying goodbye to my mother or my stepbrother and sisters or even my stepfather. I didn't at that time even know where we were going, having no idea that we were a group of migrants being sent to fill up Australia, and start a new life there. Something that I also later discovered was that it had been arranged by the governments of England and Australia.

CHAPTER TWO

Unawares to Roy and I, plans had been made by my parents with the local authorities to send us to Australia. Having very little memory of the outward journey other than always clinging to Roy, I do remember our arrival although there were only a few in our group. There were several other groups, children from different parts of England, and of all different ages and, I now know, travelling with different church organisations. I remember chaos in this big building with adult voices shouting out, 'All girls this side please and boys this side.' Many of us who were brothers and sisters or even just friends were separated by these adults. I remember being literally pulled apart from my brother Roy and seeing him dragged off one way and me being taken another way, crying, and screaming, and trying so hard not to take my eyes off him, for I knew the minute I did, he would be lost to me, lost forever. I watched him disappear into the 'boys' group' while I was put on a bus with the girls' group. We all sat terrified and listened to this adult person telling us that we were going to a children's home, and as long as we did as we were told then everything would be all right. I couldn't believe that anything would ever be 'all right' ever again. I had lost my brother, I didn't know where my mother was and I felt so lost and alone I began to cry.

I soon found out that crying didn't help at all; it only made things worse. We arrived at a place I can only describe as strange. We were all asked to line up in front of this building, a bit like being back at school. I began to remember some of my schooldays back in England and I remember really liking school. One of my teachers in particular, Mr Taylor, who used to say that I was a ' clever little girl', but that was all gone now, but where was it all gone? I couldn't understand what was happening; I only knew that was all then and this was now and here we were all stood in line, feeling very frightened and confused. We were introduced to Mr & Mrs Peterkin (who were described as head of the home) and then with our newly appointed house parents we would be put into different houses according to age. It was in 'my house' that I met Vanya who was to become my best friend and we became inseparable. We were shown to our dormitories after supervised bathing had taken place, then we all knelt beside our beds to say prayers and after getting into bed the lights were switched out and there was a firm warning of, 'No talking after lights out.'

I remember lying there frightened, as we all must have done, I could hear some of the others crying softly and others whispering. I had been used to lying in bed at night afraid and lonely but this time was much worse, knowing that my mother would not be there to comfort me, and that Roy wouldn't be there in the morning either. I didn't cry myself to sleep, but I lay there very still, watching the new shadows on the wall, feeling very sad and very afraid.

There was of course a routine to the home. We were woken early each morning at six o'clock to do allotted chores before we went to school. Sometimes it would be helping in the kitchen, or sweeping the verandas, or cleaning the toilets or dormitories and we all automatically stripped our own beds each morning and made them again for that night. Those who wet their beds were made to stand by them and they got six of the best. This meant that the house master would ask you to bend over the bed and he would beat you with a strap, cane or piece of lino, six times across the bottom, and if you put your hands in the way you would get six more. Luckily I didn't revert to bed-wetting but I did get six of the best on many occasions for talking back.

I was perhaps one of the lucky ones as I had already had a hard childhood which stood me in good stead and I just seemed to take beatings and discipline as the norm. We were introduced to our nearby school and all wore the same frocks, blue or yellow check, and we never wore shoes. The children's home had a first-aid room that was called 'surgery' and every night between certain hours you could go there and get minor ailments seen to. The most popular of these ailments would be mosquito bites or stone blisters. With mosquito bites they would douse us in calamine lotion and with the stone blisters they would put a needle through a match flame to sterilise the needle and then push it through the blister on our foot causing it to burst and all the water to flow from it. Then it would be doused in iodine. Sometimes the stone blisters would be bigger than a tenpence piece. After a while our feet became very hardened to their new surroundings and so the blisters became less and less troublesome.

In the long school summer holidays we would go and stay at a 'beach home' called Coogee Beach. The rules were very much the same but there was, I remember, a huge beautiful white-sanded beach on the opposite side of the road and most afternoons if we were not in the punishment block we were escorted to the beach for a swim. Of course, at first, many of us couldn't swim but this made no difference. We were all given two minutes to get in the water or we were thrown in so we all learnt to swim very quickly, some the easy way, and some the hard way. In the long hot summers, we all slept outside on the verandas that surrounded the home and when lights were out those of us who had now been here for quite a while began to get a little braver and we would dare each other to get out of bed and run around the field in front of us without making a sound. This we all knew was quite impossible because of 'Double Gees', which were six-sided hard wooden thorns, that would stick in your bare feet and make you yelp like a scalded cat. Then the house parent would hear you and order you to stand by your bed for six of the best. We would also go on boat trips to Rotnest

Island and play sliding down the huge steep white sand dunes. On one occasion, I stood on a piece of broken bottle and ended up with a nasty cut in my foot and had to attend the hospital for stitches when I got back. There never seemed to be any urgency about anything; everything was dealt with when they were ready to.

Back at the main home, we would all have our one main meal, teatime, in a main dining hall. I can only describe it as a large canteen, but a canteen with a difference. In most canteens there is always a lot of noise going on but in this one you could hear a pin drop. There was a strict, 'no talking' rule, and, if you were caught talking often, you would be led out of the building by the ear and made to wait outside and when you went back to your 'house' you would be punished. In the main dining hall there would be a 'mail call' every evening and if there was a letter for you they would call out your name. You would then stand up and walk up the long aisle to the top table and collect your mail. My name was called out on one particular occasion and thinking I had a letter from my mother who had written to me, but not very often, I stood up and walked the long distance to the top table trying to look the bee's knees in front of all the boys, even though we were very drably dressed and we all looked the same. Some would whistle, some would jeer, and from the corner of my eye I could see some house-masters clipping some of the kids around the head or marching them out by the ear. Always keeping my eyes to the front for fear of not getting my letter, I reached the top, only to be told that I was wanted in the office that evening at seven p.m.

Walking back to my seat seemed to take forever, and shaking and trying hard to hold back the tears of disappointment, I sat down and before I could open my mouth to explain to Vanya sitting beside me I received a clip around the ear with a whispered but forceful 'No talking'. Outside the main dining hall that evening, we were all chatting and my friends were all curious as to what I was wanted in the office for. Although curious too, I could not stop myself from shaking, trying hard to remember if

I had done anything wrong, and I couldn't remember anything. I turned up at the office at seven p.m. as requested, knocked on the door, and a voice answered, 'Come in.' It was Mrs Peterkin, the head of the homes wife. We hardly ever saw her but Mr Peterkin was a monster, she more like a timid mouse. I was asked to be seated and to listen as she then turned on the radio and after a few minutes I heard the voice of a choirboy. He sang like an angel and we often heard them in church on Sundays. We both sat silent until the singing had stopped and she then turned the radio off. 'Do you know who that was, Susan?' she asked.

I answered very nervously, and said, 'No, Miss,' and she replied:

'That was Roy, your brother.' Immediately I could feel the tears well up in my eyes and I remember trying hard not to cry in case I would be shouted at and sent away. I said nothing, and she then went on to say that Roy had been in several children's homes and was always running away and causing trouble. He was now with a foster family in Melbourne and was singing in a church choir but she didn't give any more information about where he was except, she went on to say, that he had been a bad example to the homes and had always been punished for causing trouble and what a shame it was that he wasn't more settled like me. Lots of other things were said about the good of the homes that were supposedly there to help children like us and how lucky we were and that we should appreciate all the help we were given and then she ended very abruptly by saying, 'You can go now, Susan, that will be all.'

All I can remember is that I wanted to ask, 'Where is he?' I kept saying it over and over in my mind but the words would just not come out and I stood up and left. I really felt like I had been tortured and when I got back to the house everyone said that I should have asked where my brother was but we all knew that they would have been just as silent as I was.

We were allowed to write home to our families but all letters sent out and letters that came in were opened and read. I have found out since that many of my letters to my mother had comments written on the bottom like, 'Susan has everything she needs, please don't send anything' and, 'Susan is very happy here in Australia'.

At the summer home, Coogee Beach, meal times were somewhat different. There was a Mr & Mrs Logan in charge and as the home was much smaller, they, with a cook and a few helpers seemed to run it on their own. Mrs Logan was very nice to us all but we didn't see her very often, it was Mr Logan who was always lurking around every corner. He was also very fond of 'little girls' which we were all very quick to find out and were terrified whenever he came near us. At meal times he would sit in a large window seat behind the kitchen and watch us eat and he would make sure that everyone of us ate everything that was put in front of us. On several occasions we were given stew for dinner and I hated the big lumps of fat in this stew. Dinner would start at about midday and I would still be sat at the table at six o'clock with a plateful of cold congealed stew in front of me and he would still be sitting in his window box watching me, and he would almost be grinning and taking pleasure out of me, this small girl who was crying and sobbing and choking on every mouthful of food. He would also be wearing shorts and I would notice that his private parts were exposed from these loose fitting shorts but I don't know whether other girls noticed this as I did, because we never discussed it. We didn't understand at the time and we only knew that when he came near us we couldn't bear him to touch us. Yet he was always touching us in places we felt were not right. At about six-thirty I would still be at the table and he would tell me to take my dinner to the kitchen and I would be given it for breakfast. I was then sent to bed, and punished either by six of the best or no swimming for a week.

Sometimes, whilst all of us sat at the meal table, we were able to quickly remove food from our plates and wrap it in paper or our clothes and get rid of it when we left the table, but it would mean severe punishment if we were ever caught; I can still remember the screams from many who were. We would also be given two pink powdery tablets once a week at the end of the meal-time. We were told they were to keep us loose although we didn't know what that meant then, but these tablets were foul-tasting and large to swallow. We were closely watched when they were given out, and more often than not had to endure the taste. I always seemed to heave and feel sick when I swallowed them and I would then get a hiding for making disgusting noises and still have to swallow them. We nicknamed the tablets 'Apple a-days'.

Also, during the long school holidays, a day was appointed for us all to line up in the dining hall for what was known as 'outside inspection'. People from outside the home would come into the home, walk down the line of children and choose who they would like to take out for a week or sometimes two weeks. I always remember Vanya and I holding hands really tightly and promising each other never to let go and that way we hoped that whoever chose us would take the two of us. We couldn't bear the thought of being separated and sometimes we wouldn't get chosen at all and we would spend our whole school holiday in the home but on this day this kindly faced couple touched us on the shoulder and said, 'We will take these two.'

It turned out that they were both doctors, he a surgeon and she a general practitioner and they were so very kind to us. Vanya and I were just ten years of age and this was the very first time in my life that I felt happiness. Of course it was only for a very short time but the two doctors soon became known to Vanya and I as Auntie Phyllis and Uncle Phil. They lived in a beautiful home and had some lovely friends whom they always introduced to us and I remember they also had two golden spaniels named Brandy and Whiskey. We spent some very happy days with them and they would always give us things to take back to the home with us like chocolate, fruit, clothes and toys. Many of the children were given things from their holiday families but it was always taken from us when we returned and we were always told it would be shared out equally although most of the things, with the exception of some fruit, we never saw again.

CHAPTER
THREE

Life went on much the same for another year. The routine of the home was unchanged but it was always the summer holidays we looked forward to the most. Sometimes, the doctors would say they were very busy and we would only be able to stay with them for a short time but even a short time was wonderful for us.

Then, the worst thing that could ever happen to me happened. Vanya's mother had arrived from England to collect her from the home and take her outside to the big wide world to start a new life. Vanya had always said to me that her mother would come one day and take her back. It wasn't that we didn't believe her but we all would say the same thing. It was really a race to see whose mother would turn up first and it was a sort of dream, and now her dream had come true. For Vanya it was wonderful, for me it was devastating, and it all happened so quickly. One minute she was there, and, the next minute she was gone. I can't even remember saying goodbye to her but I do remember feeling that my world had fallen apart. Once again I felt afraid and very alone and I do remember going to the swing area where Vanya and I would spend all our free time and I got on one of the swings and began to swing higher and higher. We always used to say, 'See if we can go over the bars', the bars meaning the top bar to which the chain of the swing would be attached. As I was swinging higher and higher I started to sing the song that Vanya and I would sing...

Goodbye, Mummy Darling, I miss you
Just like the stars that miss the sky
Although we had to part
You're always in my heart
Goodbye, Mummy Darling, goodbye.

I still remember the tune and sing it to this day. I was crying and crying, and just wanted to swing away into the clouds, forever and ever.

Of course, life did go on for me without Vanya. I was in a children's home and there was no escape, nowhere to go. Auntie Phyllis and Uncle Phil still came and took me out but not so often, it seemed, and sometimes they would take another child to keep me company, but it was never the same as it was with Vanya. I didn't seem to be happy any more after she had left. Horrible things were still happening in the home; Mr Logan the house-master was always molesting the girls and, unfortunately, I was one of them. Then I remember another family taking me out during a holiday period. They had two young boys about my age and they all lived on a sheep farm. When I first got there it was fabulous. I loved the freedom and the open spaces and having the use of my first bicycle to get around the farm with. I had never seen a bicycle before, let alone ride one but when you're young everything seems so easy to learn and it wasn't many hours after my first attempts and a few grazed knees that I had mastered bike riding.

We used to get up really early each morning and ride to the shearing sheds and watch all the sheep-shearers arrive to do their day's work. It was more than a day's work though as they would arrive at dawn and not leave until dusk. When I was younger it all seemed like fun, but, now when I look back I realise what a long hot, dusty and backbreaking job it was. But at the time, for me, it was pleasure. We would help sort the wool—all the old dirty bits from the underneath of the sheep and on the outside of the sheep all kept separate—and I remember on the inside of the coat of wool it was pure white and all crinkle-cut smooth and oily. The smell was not unpleasant; in fact, I remember it being a nice warm, belonging smell. I had such fun on that farm with those two boys but, as always, something had to spoil it. The husband, father of this family, began to touch me and fondle me and I hated it. I can remember being so frightened that I became very withdrawn and, suddenly, went from being a bright and bubbly girl, who was having so much fun, to a dull, frightened, moody girl. The change was very noticeable and the mother asked me why. I didn't say for fear I would be blamed and quickly answered that nothing was wrong, but I think she guessed. Then I heard them, the parents, arguing, and the next thing I knew I was bundled back in the truck and taken back to the home. I never even said goodbye to the boys or my new-found friends or anyone else. I felt like I was being punished and once again I felt very sad and alone.

My schooldays were enjoyable and I have in my possession to this day a school report that was apparently sent to my mother in those days saying, 'Susan is doing very well at school and enjoys good health.' We went to an outside school and that was nice as we were able to mix with other children although sometimes it was awful because the other children knew we were from a children's home and could use it to be cruel to us. They often did and they would call us 'you homies' and, of course, we couldn't deny it as we all dressed the same. Generally, school was good and I remember when the weather got very hot we were allowed to go home from school if the temperature reached 100 degrees. When the thermometer hovered around 98 degrees we would breathe heavily on it and the hand would climb to 100 and the alarm bell would go off. Mostly we would get away with it and all be sent home and even though 'home' wasn't much for me it was all I knew, and memories of my real home in England were fading now. I used to lie in bed at night and trace round and round Roy and my mother's face over and over again in my mind so as not ever to forget them, but gradually the images were fading.

Life continued and, if we behaved and stayed out of trouble,

18

everything became bearable. There was nothing to compare with because it was all we knew. Another memory of that time was when I was given a job in the kitchen helping the cook. There were always about five of us to help in the kitchen before and after school duties (as they were called). We would prepare the vegetables, stir the custard in a huge pan, and every morning really early there would be a huge cauldron on the stove, full of milk being brought to boiling point. It would then be allowed to cool and then one of us would have to scoop all the cream that had settled on the top into a dish; then that was put aside for some other use and the boiled milk would be used for our breakfast, which was always bread and milk. I remember it being horrible at first but after eating it every day it seemed to grow on us and we all got to like it. Cooks came and went and we never seemed to have the same one for very long; I don't know why. I do remember on one occasion watching a cook with only half an arm, a very nice person, using her half-arm to hold the carrots and vegetables and chop with her other hand. It is something that really sticks in my mind because it made me feel sick when I watched her and to this day I feel very nauseous about any physical deformity.

There were always thousands of creepy-crawlies and they would crunch under our bare feet in the dormitories when we were going to bed but that never seemed to bother us. We were allowed some free play-time but always in the grounds, of course, with very strict orders as to the boundaries. I was always very fond of playing with dolls and the grounds were very 'outback' in appearance and there were lots of little rock crevices which we would fill with water and bathe our dolls and wash their clothes. We would play all sorts of games, one very popular game being 'five stones' and skipping was also very popular. We would have two girls, each holding one end of the rope and they would turn the rope and one of us would run in and skip and sing, 'I call in my best friend and her name is Vanya, here she comes washing her clothes, and here she comes touching her toes,' and we would all do the actions and keep on at it until one tripped on the rope and was out. Hopscotch was another favourite pastime and we would use a stone as chalk to chalk out the squares. Marbles was also popular but it was always difficult to get the marbles and mostly we would win them at school playing other games.

I was fast reaching fourteen now, but was still very naïve, probably more like seven-year-olds today. We moved up the line as we got older, moving into different 'houses' according to our age. We watched and often jeered the new girls that arrived especially when they were covered from head to toe in mosquito bites, all red and sore-looking. We were all told not to scratch, but you couldn't help it, especially at night when they would drive you mad. Now it was the turn of the new girls because after a few months somehow we built up an immunity to the 'mozzies' as we called them and then we would say we were 'true Australians'. Anyone enduring mozzie bites was still a 'pom' and had to wait until they were completely clear of bites before they became an Aussie. I have memories of some of the girls being as old as seventeen or eighteen and they would go 'outside' to work, coming back afterwards. We always used to say that we would never come back, that we would run away if we got out, but, looking back now, there were no six-foot-high walls or barbed wire because there was simply nowhere else to go. There were girls who had tried and many from the boys' quarters who ran away but they were always brought back and very severely punished.

Looking back now I see we were supplied those needs that were essential to us and that was all: there was no love, no one to hold us, no one to listen and no one to tuck us into our beds and kiss us goodnight.

I remember once again being summoned to the top table at evening meal-time and although I was far from being 'street-wise' I was very 'home-wise' by now, being known as one of the oldies. I was asked to report to the office at around seven-thirty.

I tried my best to recall if I had broken the rules. Had I done something wrong? Was it Roy?—who by this time was just a distant and very faint memory in the back of my mind. Or had I been caught jumping the fence with a group of girls trying to get sight of the boys. I was fourteen now and very much aware of my body developing, and I always seemed to have a flirty side to me. What could it be I asked myself again? I hadn't had a letter from my mother for ages now but I never did get very many from her and somehow it didn't seem to bother me at the time. I didn't know her; I couldn't remember much about her and some of the girls used to be cruel and say, 'I bet you haven't really got a mother.' Yet I was quick to retaliate: 'I have so,' I would say, but all the time wondering to myself, did I have a mother? I couldn't relate to a place called England and always felt that I had been born in this place and that I would die in this place.

I attended the office as ordered, knocking on the door, shaking, feeling very scared. It was Mr Peterkin this time, the head of the home who I can describe as huge, towering above me—a big scary man with black hair, just like a giant and very angry-looking. 'Sit down,' he said and started to ask me if I was happy in the home and did I like living in Australia, and who were my friends and my house-master? But I found it very hard to relax; I had heard such monstrous stories about this man, especially about his behaviour to the boys—how he would beat them, bang their heads against the walls, and punish them in this way for the least little thing. So I didn't take my eyes off of him and I just answered, 'Yes, sir,' or, 'No, sir.' He then produced a pack of letters tied together with a string and went on to say that these were letters from my parents telling me that I might be returning to them in England.

I must have sat there mouth agape because no words came out and he then said that he knew that Roy, my brother, had been found stowing away on a ship that he'd thought was going to England but in fact had ended up in Victoria. He went on to say that the Australian authorities had had more than enough trouble from my brother and that the Australian government was sending him back to England—deporting him, he said. My parents had been informed and apparently my mother had said that Roy had a sister in Perth and she wouldn't have one child back without the other. I later learnt that the Australian government had asked my parents to pay over four hundred pounds for our return fare and my parents had said that they didn't have anything like that kind of money and couldn't pay. So, I had been summoned to his office, now, for him to ask me if I really wanted to go back. He went on to say that I was a model citizen for Australia and they wanted to keep children like me to fill up Australia and that he had held my letters back, after reading them, until he was sure that I might be going back. He did everything to try and persuade me to stay in this 'Bright and New Country' as he put it and he said that whatever I decided I was not to discuss it with the other girls for fear of putting notions into their heads.

He asked me, once more, 'Do you want to stay or return?' and everything seemed to come back to me. My mind was swimming and all I could seem to think of was seeing my brother Roy again but it didn't seem to matter that I would be going home. This was my home—I just wanted to be with Roy. It was just like I had been asked to go on a trip to see my brother; nothing else registered with me. I hadn't seen him for nearly four years and we would have so much to say to each other. In my mind I still saw him as a small boy and I remember trying to form a picture of him in my mind but every time that I nearly got there the image would disappear. I felt a gush of excitement run through my body as I sat there and I could still hear Mr Peterkin talking but I couldn't hear anything he was saying. After what seemed hours he stood sharply to his feet and said, 'Well, have you decided?' and thinking only of Roy, I said, 'Yes, sir.' I was then told that plans would be made for me and I would be notified.

'You may leave now,' he said and I remember walking from the office on a platform of air although I was still feeling very shaky and frightened though the fear didn't seem to control me like it used to. I walked back to the house and all the time I kept going over and over in my mind what was happening in case it was all a dream. It felt like a dream but maybe that's how I wanted it to be. I had always been a frightened child; maybe I just got by on dreams since reality always scared me. I think what I am trying to say is that life was so mundane then, so routine, that having something else to think about, without even having to do anything, just made things different. Now, in retrospect, I suspect, it was a deep inner fear of facing reality for fear it would be snatched from me again. I remember skipping back to the house, faster and faster and several of my friends were there waiting for me to return: if there was any excitement going on we all needed to know about it. I knew that I had been told not to say anything to the others so I remember making them swear themselves to secrecy so that they wouldn't say a word—because there was no possible way that I could keep this to myself. They all held their hands in the air and said after me, 'I swear, on the holy Bible.' Then I told them. I didn't have one special friend at that time because after Vanya had left nothing ever seemed to be the same, so I just became one of a group of friends.

After I had told them, everyone started to ask questions, 'What was old Peterkin like? Were you scared? Did he hit you? When are you going, you lucky ducks?' We were all so excited that we were working ourselves up to a near frenzy when we heard a shout from our house-master: 'What are you girls up to? Come on, there is work to do,' and we all gradually dispersed, with me reminding each one of them that they had sworn on the Bible not to tell.

From that day, life never got back to normal although there was nothing for me to do to prepare for my departure. We never had any belongings that were our own: all our clothes were put into the laundry when worn, and came out altogether and we would just take another dress from the pile or a set of underclothes because everything went round in a cycle. We had a few toys—small dolls, or something we had made ourselves—but we always shared them with each other and many times swapped them simply just to have a change. I can remember plaiting grass stems together to make ties for our dolls' hair or making clothes for our dolls out of leaves—almost anything we could get hold of. Sometimes we would sneak into the mending room and get a few pieces of material or cotton but we knew what would happen if we got caught. Six of the best wasn't our biggest fear any more as our bottoms must have hardened to it. Our biggest fear was losing our fun-times such as swimming, or going on an outing, and instead being sent into the dormitory to spend all day alone; that was far worse. The chatter and excitement died down after a while and things all got back to normal. It was several weeks now and I hadn't heard a thing about leaving and probably because I treated it like a dream it didn't seem to bother me. Little did I know that what was to be the second biggest change to my life was waiting just around the corner.

I can't recall what day of the week it was; I only know that I was taken this time to the main hall office to see Mr & Mrs Peterkin. I was given a once-over inspection—clean dress, hair combed and tied back with a hairclip. All our hairstyles were very similar; looking back now on photos I can see they were what was known as the 'basin cut'—cut straight round, level with the bottom of your ears. 'Right, follow me,' came the instructions from the house-master. 'And remember, only speak when you're spoken to.'

As we got closer to the office which was approximately a third of a mile away I began to tremble and I could feel my stomach turning over. Suddenly, I felt I didn't want this change, I wanted to go back to the house where I always felt safe, even though I never felt happy there. I had never felt really happy since that day at the fair with Roy. That had been the happiest day of my life even though I was punished at the time. Right this minute, as we approached the office I could see the horses on the roundabout going up and down and Roy, on the dodgem cars, smiling and waving to me as he went past.

Suddenly I felt a sharp smack around the back of my head. 'Susan,' said the house-master, 'where are you? You're always dreaming, pull yourself together.' I seem to recall him saying, 'You may be going home but until you do you are still in our care.'

After he had knocked on the door I was left to enter on my own. 'Come in.' The voice was that of Mrs Peterkin whom we didn't see very often. She was a very frail looking timid sort of a lady and we had given her the nickname 'Mousie'. 'Sit down, Susan,' she said, and I sat down very nervously noticing that he, he being Mr Peterkin, was sitting beside her. His nickname, used by the boys, was 'King Rat'.

He began to speak reminding me about our last meeting and what was discussed and said that before he went on to say what he had to say he wanted to ask me again to make sure. 'Do you want to go home and leave Australia?' he said.

'Yes, sir,' I answered, thinking to myself that I must have appeared to be like a 'mouse' at that moment. He then went on to say that arrangements had been made for me to be taken to Fremantle docks on such and such a day and there I would be reunited with my brother Roy and we would board the SS *New Australia* bound for England. Once again I stood there mouth agape and I couldn't believe my ears. 'That will be all,' he said. 'Your house-master will be instructed to make the arrangements for you to leave.' Little did I know that that was to be the last time I ever walked from that office and the last time I saw its familiar surroundings. In fact, it was the very last thing I recall of Swan Homes and I don't even remember saying goodbye to anyone.

I don't remember how much time went by or what arrangements had been made. I don't even recall travelling to Fremantle to board the ship but, oddly enough, I can recall what I was wearing. It was a bright yellow sleeveless blouse with a pale lemon full cotton skirt, the type worn in the 'fifties, and I distinctly remember wearing a white daisy shape 'pop-up' belt. All the pieces of it would pop together so if it was too big you could take a few daisies out and still the others would pop together. I was also wearing shoes and I remember they were ugly, big brown things. 'Clodhoppers' is the expression that comes to mind. I suppose they had to be big because not having worn shoes for so many years my feet had become hard and spread out and I remember I was also wearing white socks. I felt like a beauty queen. I had never ever seen, let alone worn, clothes like this before. My hair was short and sort of curly and always had a natural kink to it and most mornings I used to damp it down with water. The house-master would often say I looked like a waif and stray and send me back to the dormitory to 'do something about your hair'. But, this day it was quite natural and there was nobody there to tell me otherwise. It was almost like feeling I had been cast out from somewhere, that I wasn't wanted any more and it made me feel so nervous. I couldn't see what I looked like in a mirror as there were only small facial-size mirrors in the shower rooms and we were always told that we would grow up too vain if we were looking in mirrors all day. At that time we didn't even know what 'vain' meant and we would just obey, and say, 'Yes, miss,' or 'No, miss,' or whatever was expected of us at the time.

Mrs Peterkin had gone shopping and bought me these new clothes and arranged the packing of my suitcase. She was always very quiet when around any of us but we never really relaxed for fear of Mr Peterkin. She had also arranged to take me to the docks and I only have very vague memories of sitting with her in a vehicle of some sort to get there.

My memories came flooding back on arrival at the docks. I remember all the hustle and bustle and there seemed to be people everywhere, I had never seen so many people. I had seen hundreds of children at main meal times in the dining room but I had never seen so many grown-ups. I was taken to a lady in a white uniform and hat and was introduced, being told that this lady was a purser officer, who was going to look after me on board the ship until I got to England. Mrs Peterkin then left me with a quick, 'Well, goodbye Susan, be a good girl; and a credit

26

to Australia,' and with a very abrupt tap on the shoulder she left. I was too excited to make anything of it or to think of all those past years. I was even too excited to think where I was going; all I could think of was seeing Roy again.

I kept looking about for him, waiting for him to come running up to me, yank me by the arm and the two of us would run off holding hands without a care in the world. I kept thinking of all the fun we would have together again. We could go to the fair again and laugh and joke and he could play as many tricks on me as he liked and I wouldn't mind as long as we were together. The 'come on then, Susan' voice from the purser woke me from my day-dreams and I found myself being dragged through the crowds of people. After a short visit to an office on the dockside she asked, 'Would you like to go on board now, Susan?'

'Will Roy be there?' I asked.

'Oh yes,' she said, 'your brother.' She went on to explain that we would find our cabin first, then get our luggage sorted and put away, and finally we would go and find Roy. She had a kind face, although she didn't seem to know much about me, and after a while I began to realise that anything I asked for she would say yes to. However, my requests were only small; although I was now fourteen and a half years old then, I realise now, that living in the children's home all that time our bodies may have grown up but our minds hadn't, not very fast anyway.

She said I was to share a cabin with another girl of similar age; her name was Elaine, and she would introduce her to me later. 'Find somewhere to put your clothes away,' she said, 'and I will pop back later so we can go and find your brother.'

It was all so scary but I felt so excited I wasn't going to let fear spoil it. I looked around the cabin and there in front of me was 'me' in a full-length mirror. I could see a whole picture of me and I started to twirl this way and that way, making all sorts of different poses—smiling, frowning, twisting and turning. I really felt like a queen and, now, I looked just like a queen. It wasn't long before there was a knock on the door and the purser stood there with a young girl. 'This is Elaine,' she said, 'and this is

Susan.' We smiled at each other, shyly, and the purser added, 'I will leave you for a while to get your things sorted,' and off she went again.

I didn't know anything about Elaine and didn't know whether she knew anything about me either but it didn't seem to matter. I went straight into a sort of giggly, chatty conversation with her, telling her that I was going to meet my brother, Roy and how excited I was, and we jumped up and down on the beds laughing and giggling and I started to shout out, 'I'm free, I'm free.' Elaine joined in but I don't think she quite understood what I meant, but I did. Deep down inside me somewhere I felt like a little moored rowing boat that had been tied to the shore and someone had come along and cut the rope and, like the little boat, I was floating along feeling so free.

There wasn't much in my suitcase to unpack, as I had no personal belongings. I didn't even have the doll that I had grown so attached to in the home, the rule being if anyone left, they left their toys to the house and we were told it would teach us not to be selfish and enable us to share with others. It took me but a few minutes to put the things away from the case, there only being a few toiletries, and a second change of clothes. I did recognise the suitcase as being the same one that I had travelled out to Australia with—my name and all the tickets were still intact—and I began to picture in my mind this huge room piled high with suitcases that the home must have kept, belonging to all the children in the home. Both Elaine and I had unpacked and were messing around trying all the fancy things in the cabin, flicking switches and generally being giggly girls when someone knocked on the door again and in walked the purser with—I know now, but didn't at that moment—my brother, Roy.

'Susan,' she said, 'this is your brother Roy.' I looked up at this very tall 'man' and couldn't believe my eyes. For a split second my thoughts raced to the past, not appreciating that my brother had grown into a young man. I had half expected to see a young boy come running at me to go out and play with him. When I had brought my mind back to reality, Roy spoke to me in a deep voice: 'Hello Susan.' I felt almost too embarrassed to answer so I ran to him as I was still very much a child and hugged him, and hugged him until I thought I was going to burst.

His arms went round me and he lifted me into the air. 'Hey there,' he said, 'don't get all upset, don't cry, we are back together now and I'll look after you.' Together we had by now unblocked the doorway and were all in the cabin when the purser said, 'Come on, Elaine, you come with me; we'll leave them together for a while; I'm sure they have lots to tell each other,' and with that they left.

I remember I couldn't stop chattering and I don't think I let Roy get a word in because I must have asked him hundreds of questions. I told him all about hearing him singing on the radio and how Mrs Peterkin had sent for me. Then he started to tell me all the different places he had been, and all the adventures he had had whilst running away from different homes. Anything I had to tell him soon fell into insignificance as he had had such an exciting and very scary time. But I didn't care now about the past—we were back together again after nearly four years and that was all that mattered. I remember saying to him, 'Roy, can I pinch you to see if you are really there and that this is not a dream?' So we both set about pinching each other and rolled about laughing. You see, he was still my little brother—just that he was now in a much bigger body.

We had been together for almost two hours now and not once had we mentioned to each other the reason we were back together—we had even forgotten that we were on a ship. Suddenly, he looked up at me and said, 'Susan, what do you think about us going home?'

At first I didn't want to answer him. I didn't want this lovely moment to end and I didn't want to be back in the real world. I wanted to stay like this with Roy for ever and ever.

Again he said, 'Well, what do you think?'

I said I didn't understand, that I didn't know what he meant, or anybody meant, by going home. Going home to me was being with him and he laughed a little, then said, 'You know, back with Mum and Dad.' I didn't know, or I didn't want to know, I just didn't want to talk about it.

Elaine came back into the cabin and I introduced her properly to my brother. I felt so proud of having a big brother to show off. Roy said he would show me where his cabin was and that I could go there anytime and that I was to be careful on the ship as there were lots of 'troops' on board because even though the Suez Canal Crisis was over it was still all a bit uncertain. I didn't know what he meant but I said, 'OK, I will.' It just felt wonderful that he cared for me.

I remember the next six weeks very well. It was, to say the least, eventful. Being fourteen and a half years of age in body meant body changes and on this particular occasion I had left Roy on deck. He was busy with a girl he had met on board named Barbara. I needed to use the toilet and when I got there I noticed what I now know was my period. I panicked because I thought that I had cut myself and ran with all my might back to the place where I had left Roy with Barbara. They were still there so I barged in between them. By now the tears were rolling down my face, 'Roy, Roy,' I said, 'I've cut myself really badly.'

'Where?' was his quick reply.

'Down there,' I said, pointing at the same time. I saw Roy look at Barbara and the simultaneous look passing between them, then they sort of smiled at each other. I couldn't understand these facial expressions and I was frozen to the spot with total fear. Roy then said that Barbara would go back to the toilets with me and that there was something that she wanted to explain to me; I wasn't to worry. So off I went still feeling afraid and very confused. First, we stopped off at my cabin and she asked me to show her what I had unpacked from my suitcase. After asking her why, she sat me on the bed and started to explain to me all the facts of growing up and how the body would change from a young girl to a young woman. Barbara was a complete stranger to me but she made me feel so relaxed and after I had fully understood what she had said we even had a little chuckle to ourselves. She did find that the children's home had put a package in my case and I had just thrown it in the drawer with all the other things. I didn't know what it was but looking back now I can't believe that the children's home had obviously thought this might happen, but didn't even bother to tell me.

Life on the ocean wave had its wonderful moments and I saw whales, flying fish, porpoises and both Elaine and I had total freedom. The purser who was supposed to be my guardian was busy with one of the other pursers. Elaine, I found out later, had been one of a group of 'deportees' that were being sent back to England, very much like Roy and I. I didn't know anything else about her and to this day I have never seen her since. We didn't talk about who we were or where we were going; we were just busy having fun since we were both at a flirtatious age. With the Royal Airforce troops on board we would often run out of our cabin and flirt with them very innocently. On many occasions we would be in our baby-doll pyjamas and they would tell us off and order us back to our cabins. Never were they ever disrespectful to us and they were always perfect gentlemen.

There were several deportees on board and Roy had become friendly with some of them, introducing me to one particular one whom I remember as Stan.

Stan was very kind to me and he acted as though he were my bodyguard. He was much older than me; I would guess about twenty-five to thirty. I don't recall much about him but I do remember one incident. There was an attendant at the swimming pool below decks where we used to go and swim, and he was always trying to get me on my own. He always seemed to want to touch me and it made me remember how things were in the home. I hated it, although on many occasions I was afraid to say no in case I was punished in some way. There is something that I am not proud of now – when I was young I always seemed to want to flirt with older men; maybe this attendant got all the wrong signals from me but Stan, my bodyguard, soon sorted things out for me. I had, of course, told him all about it and he said to leave things to him and not to worry. I remember him saying, 'He won't bother you again.' The attendant never did bother me again; he never even looked at me or spoke to me after that. I don't know what Stan said or did but whatever happened it worked. So that's what I remember of Stan always looking out for me and he always behaved towards me in a very proper manner.

Because the Suez Canal situation was still news, the ship anchored off for several days before passing through. I remember the Egyptians pulling up alongside in their small boats and selling their wares. They would send up baskets with black carved elephants in them and watches, and they would accept anything in exchange: we would send down bars of soap from the ship and anything else we could get hold of. One of the passengers bought a watch and there was no working parts inside it. We would also throw small coins into the canal and they would dive in to retrieve them. They would all be talking in their own language to us so we didn't understand what they were asking for but they seemed pleased with what they got and we were more than pleased with our elephants. Sometimes there would be four or five carved elephants, from a large one to a very small one.

All the troops on board had been ordered to stay below decks just in case we were mistaken for a ship of war, and the loudspeaker had asked all civilian passengers to stay on deck, so we had all the excitement. We were eventually able to sail through the canal and everybody cheered and waved until we were back on the open seas.

On one of the very few occasions that I saw the purser who was supposed to be looking after me, she had told me that when we arrived in England our stepfather would be there to meet us. I remember asking Roy what he would look like and Roy replied that he couldn't remember but he would know him when he saw him. It didn't seem to concern me I seemed to think that this was my new life on the ship and that it would go on for ever and ever. I was so happy, it was such good fun, and there was nobody to tell me off or hurt me but I soon found out that all good things come to an end and they did.

There was great excitement on board. We had arrived in England and the ship was docking, its funnel sounding off and all the passengers were cheering. Roy and I were leaning over the railings trying to get a good look and he was scaring me and said things like, did I know there was a big hole in the side of the ship and that if we hadn't arrived when we did we would have sunk and we would have all drowned!

He was so convincing that I believed him. I always believed everything he said—he was my brother and I loved him so much and although he was always tormenting me I felt very strongly that he loved me too.

There was so much hustle and bustle on the ship, and everyone was pushing past to get off. Roy turned to me and said, 'Hold on to me tight and, whatever happens, don't let go.'

Immediately I felt afraid. I hadn't felt like that for several weeks but all of a sudden it all rushed back at me. What was happening? Where was I going?—going home I had been told but where was home? The only home I knew was far behind me now, and so were all my friends. I wondered for a few seconds what they were doing now and I began to miss them but Roy kept pushing his way through the crowds and pulling me along and I didn't dare let go of him. He kept saying to me that we must get to the cabin and find the purser—she would know what to do, and where we had to go. I just agreed with everything he said because I knew he would make things right.

We eventually reached the cabin; our suitcases—Elaine's and mine that we had packed the day before—had already gone. When I thought, 'Elaine, where is she?' I remember saying to Roy, 'I want to say goodbye to Elaine,' and he said, 'Come on, we haven't got time, there isn't anyone here,' and once again he grabbed me by the arm and tugged me and my legs started running to keep up with his. I remember very clearly feeling how eerie a ship below deck feels when there isn't anyone about. It makes you feel like there is no one left in the whole wide world except you and that you can't get out, that you are trapped, but Roy got me out, he was always my hero.

We were now on deck again and we heard our names being called out and looked over to see the purser waving her arms and calling, 'Over here.' It wasn't so crowded now and several passengers had already gone down the gangplank and just disappeared into their own lives. I never saw Elaine ever again; in fact, I never saw anyone from that ship ever again. How strange that we pass through life meeting different people and making friends and yet we often never see them again. How very sad.

This was the moment that I had not waited for. The moment that I had always ignored, blanked from my mind, the moment that I didn't want to face up to. I think if I had thought that my mother was going to be there, then I would have felt different. She had always written to me in the children's home, although not very often, and on reading her letters she had never seemed like my mother—and I couldn't picture what she looked like. I remember I used to squabble with the other girls and say things like 'my mother says she loves me' and some of them would say 'so does mine' and others would sit and cry because they didn't even have a mother. Now here we were, about to meet our stepfather. There was nothing I could do to change things and there was a little bit of excitement welling up inside me. I was with Roy and I knew he would take care of me and I was beginning to wonder what my new life was going to be like. I knew that I was going to meet two new younger sisters and a younger brother and I had tiny memories in my mind of having a brother older than Roy but no real memories of knowing anything about him.

CHAPTER FOUR

I remember being taken off the ship and taken to a waiting room where we were introduced to a short, stocky man who was sort of half smiling, and after a few thank yous and goodbyes we were on our way 'home' with him. I couldn't remember his face at all but Roy said he could remember him a little and told me not to worry as everything would be all right. He always used to say that. He said that when we went to the fair instead of going to Sunday school and he said that when we went to Australia, and we were separated for all those years but I still believed and trusted him. At this very minute I had to as he was all I had and I was so afraid and alone.

Our stepfather was asking us questions. 'What sort of trip did you have?' Roy did most of the talking and they seemed to be quite chatty with each other but I began to get flash-back memories of my stepfather, memories that were not very nice. Every time he spoke or made an attempt to hold my arm as part of hurrying me wherever it was we were going I pulled away from him or I didn't answer and very soon I think he began to suspect what I was doing. We had reached the station where we had to get a train and we were told that the journey would not be too long and that our mother and new brother and sisters were anxiously waiting to see us. The train ride was very quiet and most of the time we all fell asleep, being very tired, and all the strange goings-on were very tiring. We were all awoken with the cry of, 'Next stop Temple Meads, all those for Temple Meads station, next stop.'

'Come on,' Roy said, and we all made our way to the door. The station was very busy with people coming and going and we were making our way along the platform when a voice from behind us said, 'Hello there, can I have a chat with you, just for a minute?'

I remember my stepfather turning very quickly and before any more questions were asked he swung his arm at this man who was just about to take a picture of us, knocking the camera from his hand. It crashed to the ground, fell apart and the spool of film slipped out and uncoiled beside the broken camera. In a matter of what could only have been a few seconds, he grabbed my arm and said to the both of us, 'Run, don't look up and keep running.' He went on to say that we should have got off the train at another station and caught the bus and that way the 'reporters' would not have been waiting for us. At the time I had no idea of what was going on but I later found out that Roy and I were 'news' having been sent to Australia as 'Child Migrants' and now being sent home. They, the reporters, wanted to know why. My stepfather seemed angry and that made me remember more about him but Roy seemed to be enjoying it all. I was nervous and although I was only one month off my fifteenth birthday I was still very young for my age and very naïve.

After a very short bus ride we were at the top of the hill where the bus terminus was, where the buses would turn around and go back the other way until the end of their shift when they would pull into the depot until the next shift. We didn't have much luggage, and what we had we carried between us. 'It's not far now,' my stepfather said, 'only down this hill,' and I could feel my stomach turning over with apprehension. Now I was beginning to feel really excited and I kept saying over and over to myself, 'Will she like me? Will my mother like me?'

I remember thinking how everything looked so small and so green and all clumped up together. In Australia everything was open spaces and warm sunshine, with really high blue skies whilst here it seemed that the sky was almost resting on our heads.

'Here we are then,' he said and went through a small gate, walked up a short little path, and knocked firmly on the door. I was holding Roy's hand very tightly, tightly enough to squeeze the blood out of him but he once again looked at me and said, 'Don't worry, everything will be all right.'

The door opened and...I will try and describe the next few minutes. Our mother stood there wearing a smile that would light the world and she ran to Roy and put her arms around him with tears in her eyes—I thought she would never let him go. I stood there waiting for my turn and it seemed that I waited and waited, and although I got what only seemed to me a small hug and a kiss I hoped everything would improve later. I hoped that my turn would come.

We all seemed to go through the door at the same time and inside waiting patiently were our two stepsisters and our stepbrother. They were all over us, hugging and kissing and all at once I managed to forget all that was sad and joined in all the celebrations. It was wonderful and my mother kept repeating how wonderful it was to have us home. My stepfather was busy explaining how difficult it had been getting from the ship to the train and how we had found reporters waiting for us at the station, and what he had done to one of them. He also told my mother not to answer the front door because they would not give up that easily and would probably come to the house. I knew what he was saying but I didn't understand any of it, and didn't want to—in case whatever it was would send us away again. My new brother and two sisters were aged ten, nine and eight years and we really got on well. My mother kept asking me whether I could remember anything that happened before we went away and I would say, 'No,' and she would reply, 'Never mind, you're home now,' and we would smile at each other.

We busied ourselves that evening by unpacking our cases and giving to our parents the black elephants with ivory tusks that we had got from the men in their small boats on the Suez Canal. We gave smaller things, like bars of soap and writing paper and envelopes that we had taken from the ship to the others. The whole evening was very exciting except one small incident when someone had knocked at the front door and I remember my stepfather getting very angry and saying, 'Don't answer it, do you hear me? That means all of you, don't answer the door.' Nobody did, and eventually it stopped knocking.

The next day a small article appeared in the local evening paper. My stepfather had been scouring the pages to see if there was anything and he read out loud to my mother something about two child migrants being sent back from Australia. He seemed pretty pleased at the time that they had written very little, but then went on to say, 'Bloody nosy parkers, always sticking their nose in other people's business.' He carried on reading the rest of the paper, and the subject never came up again.

The early days that followed were still all very exciting, there being so much to tell, by Roy and me and the others. We spent hours together, playing and we didn't have to take time to get to know each other; it was as if we had known each other all our lives. With our parents, it was different and, as we began to settle in, things started to change. This was a small three-bedroom house, and now it was very cramped. Roy shared a room with Rodney, our new stepbrother, and Yvonne and Shirley were in the second bedroom but there were only two beds in their room, so I had to share a bed with Shirley, the youngest. Of course, our parents had the other room. Roy was getting restless because all the excitement had worn off now, and normal life had resumed, and it wasn't an easy life. I remember my fifteenth birthday was very near, and that it was only a few weeks until Christmas, and how hurtful it was when my mother said, 'Your birthday is so near Christmas Susan, we have decided to wait and give you your present all in one on Christmas Day.' And that's how everything had been since I had 'come home'. Everything was about Roy and I didn't seem to fit into the equation at all. Christmas came and went, and although it was fun, and sort of cosy, things were not quite right.

I had very quickly come to realise that my mother revolved around Roy whom she idolised and he could do no wrong. I was just a teenage daughter who was good for looking after the young ones or cleaning or ironing and of course I was very good at all these things having had plenty of practice in the children's home. So, my mother made use of my 'skills' but Roy, on the other hand, was her favourite and he could say or do no wrong. This, in turn, caused a lot of friction between him and my stepfather, both already noticing that there wasn't a lot of love lost between the head of the household and the newcomers. We were in his way, in his house, and the novelty had already worn off—it was very clear that he didn't want us there. We had overheard snatches of conversations with him and my mother such as, 'I don't want them teaching my kids bad habits,' or, 'When is that lazy layabout going to get work?' meaning Roy.

I had been placed in the last year of the senior school at the start of the new term after Christmas, but Roy was past the leaving age for school and was expected to get a job. To me he didn't seem ready to go out and get a job. He was still a young boy, a young boy in a grown-up body; that's how both of us were but there was no time for sentiments and we were expected to fit in. Roy became very restless and did in fact become quite moody. I had never seen him like this before, he having always been the tearaway type and it was becoming very noticeable to me that he would get angry for no reason. I say 'no reason' lightly, as both he and I knew what was wrong. He managed to get several jobs but could never seem to keep one for very long and that would anger my stepfather more and more and it had also become very noticeable that our parents were arguing all the time. 'Your kids and my kids'—that was all we could hear, day in and day out. Roy, especially, became like a carbuncle on my stepfather's back; they couldn't look at each other, couldn't even speak to each other, and this made it very difficult for my mother. She loved Roy with all her heart and although her favouring towards him at times was very obvious, she did everything she could to keep the peace between the warring males.

I was just plodding on at school doing what I was supposed to do. I did enjoy school and although I found it very hard at first I made friends easily. The other girls liked it because I was sort of different and they would ask me all about Australia and then they would say to me, 'Say something in Australian,' and everybody would laugh. It made me feel important and I suppose it was a sort of attention-seeking, but I loved people thinking I was Australian and I always felt that I was and still am Australian. Roy and I would sit for hours sometimes talking all about Australia and he would say things like, 'I'm going back there one day, you can come if you want.' He was so confused! He had never settled since we had come back and with all the arguing going on between our parents we always knew that it was because of us. So why did they want us back? We would say to each other, 'Why did they bother? They may as well have left us where we were.'

The arguing got worse; my mother had become very withdrawn and she was very nervous of my stepfather's every move. He would say, for example, that Roy had more potatoes or meat on his plate than he had. He would purposely make us wait at the table until he was ready to eat and if either one of us leaned over to help ourselves he would say that he would 'chop our bloody hands off'. My mother began to use me in retaliation for what my stepfather did to Roy and then they started to play us off against each other. Roy was her favourite and now I was to become his favourite. Although he did treat me a little better than Roy I was certainly not really a favourite to him because he didn't want either of us there and most days in his conversation with my mother he made that very clear. To him, Roy stood out like a sore thumb, Roy having blonde hair and blue eyes while all his children had dark hair and brown eyes. I also had dark hair and brown eyes so I always seemed to fit in with his family but Roy, he kept saying to my mother, was like her first husband, which was not unnatural as we were both her first husband's children. This separation of the family went on and on and the situation got worse, although, the more he tried to separate his children, as he would put it from her children, the closer we became.

Roy by this time had had enough, announcing that he was going to join the army, which seemed to please my stepfather. 'Bloody good life,' he would say. 'Make a man of you, didn't do me no harm.' We all knew including my mother, that my stepfather was glad that he was to be rid of Roy and where else better for him to go than the army...? He had served eight or nine years in the army before getting married and as far as he was concerned there was no better life. So, for once, Roy seemed to be doing something right and this gave him a boost. At long last he was getting some attention and although my mother was very unhappy about his decision she was relieved that maybe she would now get some peace, but that wasn't to be. Roy did join the army and after six weeks we all travelled down to his base camp to watch his passing-out parade and I remember sitting there, watching him and feeling so proud. 'That's my brother,' I would think to myself and glancing across at my mother I could see her face was full of pride and guessed she was thinking, 'That's my son.' Many times, since we had come home, I had seen this look of pride on her face for Roy and wished she would wear that same look for me, just once.

Roy seemed happy in the army and at the parade he introduced us to some of his new-found friends and they chatted about all the things they had learned. Although the initial training was hard it was now behind them and the best was yet to come. He had grown up so much he didn't seem to take much notice of me now. It seemed that I was just a giggly schoolgirl to him, and although this made me feel sad, for him I was so happy. I wanted him to be happy; he was my brother and I loved him, that's all that mattered to me.

With Roy away, things were a little better at home, but not much because I had also started to grow up. I was staying behind at school some nights, making excuses that I was doing extra work, when all the time my purpose was to flirt with the boys, hang around in the park, have the odd cigarette, trying to act grown up or showing off. It wasn't long before my mother found out and then there were more arguments. 'Man-mad,' she would

41

say to me, and, 'I should have left you out there in Australia,' with me wishing under my breath that she had. I can remember getting out of bed at night and sitting on the top stair listening to my parents arguing, straining my ears, trying, trying with all my might not to let the stairs creak for fear of being caught.

I left school with moderate results but was able to achieve high marks in shorthand and typing. My stepfather had always drummed it into me to get a job in an office because factory girls were just 'riffraff' and so my first employment was with an engineering company as an invoice typist. I enjoyed it but I think the reason for that was that I would have enjoyed anything that got me away from home. I was, by now, very unhappy, being more or less a Cinderella at home; my mother did everything she could to keep me in, cleaning and helping around the house. The bouts of silence around the house when I asked to go out were awful. I was never encouraged or praised for anything. Home was simply a roof over my head and food in my stomach and that's exactly how my stepfather put it, always adding that I should think myself lucky.

I remember getting my first wage packet at work and feeling so proud of myself. I almost ran all the way home only for my mother to say, 'Where's your wage packet, Susan? That goes to me every week to help towards the costs of running this house.' She would give me back five shillings (25p), two and sixpence (12½p) to spend and the other two and sixpence for my next week's bus fare. I didn't mind that so much it's just that I could remember that when Roy had started his first job he had been allowed to keep all his money but Mother would say that boys were different and they needed more money than girls did. I just knew that there was no logic in her statement, aware that it was because she favoured Roy and, although I loved Roy so much, I envied my mother's love for him.

After several months I had found myself another job much closer to home. This didn't mean that I would save the bus fare and get more money, but it did mean that I wouldn't have to leave for work so early. It was now much easier to get to work and I was still working in the goods inward department as an invoice typist, but there was a huge factory attached to this office, and sometimes I would have to walk through the factory to deliver invoices or small parcels to the goods outward office at the other end. I would find every excuse I could to do this because I knew, when I walked through, that the men would whistle. When I left home in the mornings to get ready for work I would wear a short skirt with a coloured top and white high-heeled shoes. My hair was dark with a natural wave in it and I would look in the mirror before I set off to see if I looked all right for the 'factory walk'. Sometimes, I would think my mother was right, perhaps I was 'man-mad' as she put it. Most days I had to wear the same clothes to work. I didn't have so many that I could change more often and my shoes were always gone over on the heels and most of the time I would be walking on the spikes but these things didn't seem to bother me much because I loved my job and I loved the attention that it gave me each day.

Working in the factory was one particular boy whose looks resembled those of Elvis Presley and all the girls would chase after him, me included. I remember that he would take one girl out for a few weeks then take another and so on and we would all patiently wait for our turn. My turn came and, as all the other girls would have thought, I considered myself to be the special one. It was very hard for me to get out at night, needing to make excuses and make up things like I was going to find out about night-school or invent something to do with work. Whatever excuse I gave, I did manage to get out and meet this boy. Looking back now, I can't imagine how I did such a thing as to queue up to go out with a boy just because of how he looked but I did. I was able to get out and see him about four or five times altogether. I didn't have any experience of boyfriends but I was very good at flirting—that was all—so going out with this boy was very scary for me. All my friends had been out with him so I felt that I had to follow in their footsteps in order to keep in their favour.

I remember being very shy, and afraid that he would not like me. I suppose people would say I threw myself at his feet, because that's exactly what I did, not having the sense to know that he only wanted to go out with me, just as with all the others, for one thing. I can remember that when he touched me I would have flash-backs to the past when I was in Australia and all those 'old men' would touch me. I tried to block it from my mind and stood there, rigid with fear, fear because of my hate of what he was doing to me, and fear of losing him. It was strange because at the time I didn't even know what sex was. I had heard all my friends at work laughing and giggling about it and sometimes I joined in with their laughter just to feel like one of the crowd.

Then, suddenly, it had happened to me. I can remember straightening my clothes and walking away hand in hand but nothing was said about what we had just done and he walked me back to the bus stop and we kissed each other goodnight. I got on the bus and looked back to wave to him but by this time he had gone. My thoughts at that time returned to home and what my parents would say if they ever found out what I had done. My stepfather would kill me, I thought. Before I got off the bus at the top of the hill I had asked the bus conductor the time. 'Ten-thirty,' he had said and I knew I was late. I had always had strict orders to be in by ten o'clock and my stepfather would always say, 'No good goes on after ten o'clock, my girl,' and I couldn't help thinking that this time he was ironically right.

I remember taking my shoes off and running down the hill and along the short road that lead to the house and just before getting to the gate I slipped them back on and walked slowly up the garden path looking a picture of innocence. Sometimes my stepfather would be waiting at the front door, and on this occasion he was waiting because I was late. 'Get in,' he shouted and with a sharp clout around the back of the head he repeated himself: 'Get in, get in and get your hot water bottle and get to bed and don't wake the others. I will deal with you in the morning, my girl.' I would always try and duck his blows when he lashed out

44

at me but he never missed and sometimes it would feel as if my head would come away from the rest of my body through the force of the blows he would deliver.

Morning came and all my worrying that night, as I lay trying to get to sleep, was in vain. He was up and gone to work before me. On the many occasions this happened, by the time he got home from work he would have mellowed slightly and instead of getting a real good hiding I would get a punishment. Often I wouldn't be able to go out for a week or have to do extra chores around the house.

Going to work the day after this particular episode, I joined the rest of the girls, giggling, and told them all about my date with this boy. One girl looked up and said it was like 'pass the parcel'. Then the others asked me what he was like, though, of course, I never told them what I actually did with him. None of the other girls had ever said that they had done anything; all we did was keep swooning over the way he looked. I never went out with him again. I didn't even realise then that he had got what he came for and so he had gone on to the next girl.

Several weeks passed and everything was the same, at home and at work, when I began to sense that something was not quite right. I was late getting my period and I was frequenting the toilet much more than usual. I didn't know what was happening to me but after missing two periods I began to put two and two together. I didn't know much about the birds and the bees but I did know that I was pregnant—call it a woman's instinct, but I knew. I started to feel sick in the mornings and it was all I could do to hide it from everybody. I still shared a bedroom with my younger sisters so I had to be careful that I didn't say anything to them or do anything that they would consider to be unusual because I knew they would tell my parents: not vindictively but just because that's what younger brothers and sisters do. I was very scared; in fact I was terrified and I could now hear my stepfather's voice bellowing at me, 'Don't you dare bring home any filth here my girl, you bring home any trouble and I will kill you.'

45

I remember trying to figure out what to do but I knew I couldn't tell my mother—she would be too terrified of what my stepfather would say and I didn't feel that she cared for me much. Somehow I thought if I ignored it, it would go away. I could have told Roy but he was away in the army. He only wrote home once but that was only because my mother had made him promise to write. He hadn't said much in his letter only that things were pretty much the same and I got a small mention at the end—'give my love to Susan', and a few kisses. I had heard my parents arguing again recently about Roy, my mother saying he wanted to come home and my stepfather becoming very angry and calling him a weakling and saying the army would do him good, make a man of him. I knew it was because he never wanted Roy back home again, saying that the pair of us were nothing but trouble, and he didn't want us mixing with his children, teaching them bad habits. I can remember fantasising and touching my stomach and saying to myself, 'If I have this baby, nobody will take it away from me. Nobody will hurt it and I will love it forever and ever and run away if I have to.' Then I would say over and over, 'I hate him, I hate him,' always referring to my stepfather. I never once said I hated my mother and although I was always sad that she never loved me, I could never hate her.

A few days later a knock came on the door. 'Get that,' my mother shouted out, so I answered the door.

'It's for you, Mum, two army men,' I said.

I saw the look of terror on her face and she came to the door, still wiping her hands in her apron. 'Yes?' she said with a quiver in her voice. 'Is there something wrong?'

They told her not to worry and said that Roy had gone absent without leave from the army and wondered if he had come home, explaining that they were military police and that it was their job to find him and return him to the army. I was standing behind my mother and I interrupted and asked how long Roy had been missing. 'Never you mind,' my mother was quick to answer. 'Go inside, it's nothing to do with you.'

I knew that this was just a reaction from her associated with the panic now running through her body—concerned for Roy, yes, but terrified at what my stepfather would say and all the arguing that would follow.

The two policemen left with the promise that they would keep her informed of any news and in return she would do the same for them. Several days passed and then Roy turned up at the door. My mother went into a panic and she asked him all the obvious questions like 'Where have you been?' and 'What are you doing? Do you know that the army police are looking for you?' She begged him: 'You must go back otherwise they will send you to the army prison.'

He said he would never go back, he hated it, and he also kept saying that he didn't feel well and that he couldn't remember what he had done or what he was doing and that he kept having blackouts. My mother told me to put the kettle on and make a cup of tea but I could see that she was distraught and afraid. I knew what it was like to be afraid so I could sympathise with her.

When I brought the tea in I could see that Roy was getting angry. He started shouting and stood up and the chair fell over so he kicked it across the room and I remember my mother pleading with him to calm down and she kept reminding him that his father would be home soon and what on earth would he say? 'I don't care what he bloody says,' said Roy. 'I'm fed up caring about him. I hate him; look what he's done to you,' he said. 'You can't even love your own children,' and with that he walked out of the room, nearly knocking me over, stalked out of the front door and was gone. I put my arm around my mother to try and comfort her, knowing how hurt she was and how much she wanted to go after him but I knew that it was not my arm around her she wanted—it was Roy's, the one who she adored, and like he said, 'she wasn't allowed to love her own children'.

It wasn't long before she got notification from the army to say that they had arrested Roy and that he would be put in the army prison until things were sorted. This news seemed to make her feel more easy at the time because although he had been caught, he was safe. By this time my stepfather knew what was going on and the arguing had begun again and I hadn't even had time to think about my problem. I had no time at all to discuss it with Roy and even if I had he would have been in no state of mind to deal with it. Thus, for now at least, my secret had to remain a secret. I was still going to the bathroom about a hundred times a day, hoping with all my heart that things would change but they never did.

I somehow managed to go to the doctor one day after work and he confirmed very quickly that I was three months' pregnant. He asked the question, 'Do your parents know?' and I answered, 'No.'

He said, 'They need to know, you must tell them.'

I said I would tell them, thanked him and left. I remember I got outside and took in a deep breath of air. What was I going to do? The thought of telling my parents made me feel sick with worry and I could never imagine telling my stepfather, 'Oh Dad, by the way, I am going to have a baby.' I would rather die I thought. On my way home I tried with all my might to think of some way to tell them but I couldn't. Maybe I would wake up in the morning and it would all be a dream.

I arrived home that evening around eight o'clock only to find that my mother was waiting for me to come through the door and, as I did, I got this almighty clout around the back of the head with the words, 'You dirty hussy.' Then I received another clout. 'How could you?' she said.

'What's wrong?' I asked all innocently.

'I'll give you what's wrong,' she said. 'What's this?' and she held out my diary—well, it wasn't a real diary, just a scribble pad I had always used as a diary. 'What's this?' she screamed again, still lashing out at me. 'Your father will kill you.'

Those words rang through my ears as I realised she was only afraid of what my father would say. She didn't care about me, I thought.

'You will have to tell him, I'm not,' she said.

'Me tell him?' I turned to her, with tears in my eyes and

shouted, 'I'm not telling him, I hate him, it's nothing to do with him.'

'He's your father,' she said. 'He has to know.' Her head was in her hands. 'Oh my God,' she said, 'what are we going to do?'

I sort of quietened down and mumbled, 'Well, I'm not telling him,' and with that we heard my father coming in. He had been out to a pigeon race meeting, which was his hobby and I often heard my mother say during their arguments that he thought more of his pigeons than he did of anything else. He stood in the kitchen and asked what all the commotion was about, saying he could hear us shouting whilst he was coming up the pathway. Both my mother and I looked at each other and I could feel myself trembling.

'Well?' he asked. 'What's going on?'

'She's pregnant,' my mother replied.

'Who's pregnant? my stepfather enquired, staring at me, and coming towards me at the same time. I remember automatically raising my arm to my face and cowering in the corner, for fear of him hitting me but he didn't hit me on this occasion. Nevertheless, all hell seemed to let loose. It went on and on. 'She can't stay here,' he yelled. 'What will the neighbours think? I knew she was no bloody good, what did I tell you? I knew this would happen. We should have left the pair of them where they were,' he said. 'They have been nothing but trouble since they came back,' he went on. 'And I don't suppose she knows who the father is.'

I wanted to scream at him, 'Oh yes I do,' but I didn't dare. I just stayed frozen to the spot, until at last all the screaming and yelling died down, and my stepfather walked out of the room, but before reaching the door he turned to say again, 'She's not staying here.'

My mother told me not to breathe a word of this to the others, and that she would make arrangements for me to go away, but, in the meantime I was to go shopping for a girdle. 'We can't afford for the neighbours to see,' she said, then, 'You'd better go to bed now, you've got work in the morning, and by golly, you're

49

going to need every penny now,' and with that she too walked out of the room.

I went up to bed; my sisters were both asleep and I lay awake for hours thinking about what my parents had both said. Go away, I thought, go away where? And for a moment I thought they might send me back to Australia. My thoughts drifted back to the times in the home, wondering what everyone was doing right now and then I started to think about the time I had spent on the ship. Tears were soon filling my eyes again, and I put the bedclothes over my face so as not to make any noise and wake up my sisters, and then face a barrage of questions. Eventually I fell asleep, and awoke to face another day.

There had been no news from Roy for a while, and I desperately needed to speak with him, although I didn't think for one minute that I would be able to. I wanted to tell him about the baby, and I wanted to tell him that our stepfather had finally got his way, that I was being sent away again, which meant the two of us would be gone—gone out of his life being exactly what he wanted. My mother would remind me daily that I was a disgrace and that I had proven my father's point about teaching his own children bad habits. She also told me to contact the father of the baby and speak with his parents, and see what they had to say, if I knew who the father was.

I wrote to the father, this seventeen-and-a-half-year-old 'Elvis look-alike' just saying that I needed to talk with him urgently. I took it to work and handed it to him at the first opportunity I got and he sort of frowned at me and asked, 'What's this?'

'Just read it,' I replied and I walked away and went back to my work. I hadn't told anyone at work for fear of losing my job and I had a sort of shameful feeling about myself, so I didn't want anyone else to know. After work that evening, he was waiting for me outside but he wasn't very pleased and said that I had better come to his house and discuss it with his parents. As I looked at him I remember what my mother had said, maybe he will marry you and I thought, 'Fancy marrying someone who looks like Elvis Presley, everyone will be jealous.' Looking back now, I can see how immature I was. Arrangements were made for me to go to his house the next night so I got all dressed up, despite not owning anything too special. Although it was plain, I felt smart and even though I was rapidly putting on weight, the girdle helped to keep my tummy flat. I rang the doorbell and this tall man opened the door. 'You had better come in,' he said. I was only in the house for around twenty minutes.

'How do we know it's our son's baby?' he asked. 'You're not ruining our son's life, you got yourself into a mess, girl, you get yourself out of it.' The mother and son said nothing and it was obvious that the whole thing had been planned. I was then asked to leave and as I walked to the door he said, 'Go home now and we don't expect to hear from you ever again.'

So I did. I went home and I never contacted them or the father of my baby again. I saw him at work several times, but if I looked at him and he saw me, he would immediately look the other way and ignore me.

CHAPTER
FIVE

My mother had very quickly made arrangements to send me away to have the baby, although I don't know how she did it. I just know that, within a week or two, I was on the platform at the station waiting for a train to take me to a place called Exeter. I had with me a small bag and case which my mother had packed and I put a few sentimental things into my bag. She stood on the platform with me and as the train approached I felt that funny feeling in my stomach again, although it wasn't the baby moving. I had felt the baby several times now, and that was quite pleasant and exciting, but this time it was that fearful churning feeling that comes when you're afraid. I got on to the train and my mother said, 'Now behave yourself and don't bring any more shame on the family, and write to me.'

The train pulled away and I waved her out of sight, the tears once again welling up in my eyes. Life to me always seemed to be about crying, I thought.

An elderly lady met me at the station in Exeter, and I was taken to an unmarried mothers' home nearby. There were about twelve girls at St Nicholas House, all awaiting the birth of a child and I was introduced on arrival and very soon made friends with the others. I had been instructed to go into the nearby town the next day to look for a job, as my pay packet would be used towards the running costs of the home. Where had I heard that before, I asked myself? I wasn't a rebellious person, and most of the time I always did what I was told and I always found it fairly easy to mix with others. Looking back, I realise that I wasn't a perfect goodie-goodie and once in with the crowd I would often do silly things and be caught and punished for those things, like talking after lights out, or sneaking down to the larder to steal food for a midnight feast.

I always felt like I needed to be noticed. I was very used to orphanage life, so it didn't take long before I learnt the tricks of the trade, and it seemed that by getting pregnant, I had learnt my lesson, as my mother had once said to me. Every weekend we would go into the local town and hang around the local café to meet boys. I remember there used to be a lot of army lads in uniform, and we got chatting, played the jukebox, and had a few kisses and cuddles. They didn't seem to mind that we were pregnant. I asked if they knew my brother Roy, and on one occasion they laughed. 'Do you know how big the army is?' one of them said. 'He could be posted anywhere.' Sometimes I felt angry towards Roy, remembering that he said he would always be there to look after me, never to worry: where was he now, when I needed him most? But I could never be angry with him for long.

I wrote to my mother as often as I could, and when I got a reply from her I would read it over and over, trying to find something between the lines that would say or indicate that she loved me. They were mostly newsy letters, telling me about the others—how they missed me, and that they had asked where I was, and that my stepfather had told them that I had to go away for a while but he didn't say why, and that he had bought my mother a new iron and ironing board, which was all the rage at that time, and how he was doing with his pigeon racing, which oddly enough I was always interested in.

I had settled in well, and I was now five months' pregnant; I had a job in a shoe repair shop, serving behind the counter, so everything seemed to be going well. Then I had a letter from my mother telling me that Roy was coming home. He had been discharged from the army on medical grounds—'blackouts' she went on to say. The whole letter was about Roy; she sounded very excited. Maybe Roy will come and see me I thought, maybe he will take me away from all this and there would just be the three of us—him, the baby and me. I knew this was all day-dreaming, but as I had often found out in the past, day-dreaming—most of the time—was much better than reality for me.

I didn't get a visit from Roy, I didn't even get a letter, but my mother's letter gave me most of the news. He had come back home, got a job, and more or less kept out of my stepfather's way. The next letter I received from my mother contained news that nearly brought on the birth of my child. She talked about my elder brother Alan, and went on to say that he was at Exeter University and had promised to come and visit me. I remembered that my mother had often talked of Alan and how he was her first-born and that he had been taken by her first husband at the time of their divorce. Then he, our real father, had remarried and dumped Alan onto one of his relatives, a great aunt, who at that time was in her late sixties so Alan had thrown himself into study. The aunt was very good to Alan but far too old to bring up a young boy. It was only when I received this letter that I realised why Alan hadn't been with us in the children's home in Gloucestershire. That's why he didn't get sent to Australia with Roy and me and why we didn't really know him. My mother told me that the aunt's niece used to bring Alan up to the park, the park from where Roy and I sneaked off to the fairground instead of going to Sunday school, and my mother would meet him there and spend a little time with him—always fearful that my stepfather would catch her and try and send him away too. My mother often spoke to me of things like this but not in a close, motherly way. It was her way of dealing with her own loneliness and all her own problems. I was just a good listener simply because there wasn't much else to do at the time. Alan was older than Roy by three years, so that made him older than me by nearly six years and would make him nearly twenty-two. How embarrassing I thought! I wouldn't even know him and he would see me for the first time with my stomach swollen, being nearly seven months pregnant now. I hoped my mother had told him why I was here.

I imagined her saying, 'You had better go and visit your sister, dirty hussy has gone and got herself into a mess.' I hoped that she hadn't said these things but I began to think she would be right if she had. I was a dirty hussy and, yes, I had got myself into a mess. I had heard most of the other girls' stories and they were all of a similar kind. We were just 'girls that had gone astray'—that's how the house mistress would put it to us during meal times: 'girls who couldn't do as you were told' and that's why we were being punished.

My elder brother Alan did come to see me and in fact I was really pleased to see him. He was the only visitor I had but I didn't feel very at ease with him, not as a brother, because I didn't know him, though he did seem to be at ease with me. I remember him being very understanding and we played a game called solitaire and I remember now that he had mastered the art of never losing and was trying to teach me the same. When he left that day he asked me to keep in touch and to let him know when the baby was born and that if there was anything he could do for me to let him know. I thanked him for coming to visit me and he left.

My due date had arrived and I went into labour. I was so scared; I think more scared than I had ever been in my whole life. The pain was indescribable, and there was no way to stop it. There was a special confinement room in the home and that was where I was. I already knew quite a lot about having a baby from all the girls who had given birth before me but nothing had prepared me for this kind of pain. I cried out, but there was no one there. I felt so alone and I was only one month off my seventeenth birthday. In between the pains I tried to think why I was being punished like this or why my whole life had seemed nothing but a feeling of loneliness and sadness. I started to think about the baby I was going to have. 'Oh please God, let it be all right, I promise I won't do anything wrong ever again.' I tried to imagine what it would look like; a boy or a girl—I wouldn't mind, I just wanted it to be all right, to have all its fingers and toes, and I would love it and love it so much no one would ever take it away from me. Further pains brought me quickly back to reality and a nurse came in and examined me and said, 'It won't be long now my dear.' I can remember the radio being on and it seemed a little ironic that Elvis Presley's song 'It's Now or Never' was playing. Two hours later I gave birth to a beautiful baby girl and I held her in my arms and looked into her face and for the whole world to hear I said, 'Nobody will ever take you away from me.' I couldn't help wonder if my mother had ever said anything like that to me when I was born.

Although childbirth is pretty traumatic at the time, nature has its way of getting back to normal very quickly and it wasn't long before I was up and about caring for my baby daughter. I had named her Heidi from the story book I had read so many times and found Heidi to be such a happy little girl and beautiful, with her dark hair. Looking back now, I can see how immature I really was for a seventeen-year-old mother and I remember holding Heidi for hours and hours, just looking into her face. I would become very emotional and cry, though crying this time with joy at holding this tiny child, my child. I would repeat to myself, you are mine and no one will take you from me. Day-dreaming was something I was very good at. Yet I knew that I was a child with a child and I knew in my heart that I could not look after my child on my own. I had written to tell my parents that I had had a baby girl and that everything was all right and I went on and on saying how lovely she was. A few days later I received a letter back and I had to read it twice before I could believe what it said. 'Dad said you can come home for Christmas and bring the baby with you.' I couldn't believe my eyes! 'Bring the baby home!' He must have told everyone, my younger brother and sisters, and all the neighbours, and Roy, did Roy know? Was he still living at home, I wondered; my mother hadn't said anything in her letters lately about him but for a brief moment I felt happy.

I said goodbye to all my friends at the unmarried mothers'

home although most of them had left to go their own way. It was the kind of place where you made new friends all the time and, as some would go, others would arrive. Like Elaine on the ship, I never saw any of them ever again.

My mother was at the station to meet me and this was her first glimpse of her grandchild but there were no hugs for me just a smile and 'Is this Heidi? She's lovely.'

My mother never seemed to me to be very maternal, except to Roy that is, but it didn't matter to me now. I had my own baby and I was a mother and I would be the kind of mother that I wanted to be. When we arrived home the others were eagerly awaiting our arrival and they swarmed over the baby and, even to my surprise, so did my stepfather.

'Thank you for having me and the baby home, Dad,' I said, and he sort of grunted and said that there would be rules and no more gallivanting on my part now I had responsibilities and he wanted to see me uphold them. 'I will,' I said, 'I promise.'

They had prepared a drawer from the chest of drawers for Heidi to sleep in beside my bed that I still shared with my youngest sister. It was all very cramped, but cosy, and life more or less got back to normal. Well, that was the plan but it didn't quite work out that way. The baby would wake in the night and she would then disturb the younger ones and then my parents would start arguing about them having to get up for school and that they needed their sleep. I tried every way I could to keep Heidi from crying for too long but I was only a young girl and I soon found out that it was not all a bed of roses looking after a new baby. I had very little help from my parents. It was as if they were saying, 'You had the baby, you look after the baby.' I did try to understand that my mother already had had two families and that I didn't expect her to love me any more—just the baby. She would often remind me that it was my mistake and I must pay for it—how would I learn my lesson otherwise she would say? There were times when I thought that my stepfather had more of a soft spot, not for me of course, but for the baby.

Each day came and went, and for several weeks life went on as best it could. My mother and father would go off to work each day, and the younger ones to school. I would be at home with Heidi but I had to do all the chores, of course, in return for my keep as I wasn't a wage earner now, but I didn't mind that for I had always been used to doing housework and cooking. Roy hadn't been there when I got home, my mother saying he had met a girl and got on so well with the girl's mother he had gone to live there. I asked how he was. Fine she said, and again I got the feeling that she was happy for him and happier still that he wasn't here in the house because of the conflict between him and my stepfather, which was now much worse since Roy had been discharged from the army. That was a disgrace in my stepfather's eyes, no matter what the circumstances were, and he had told my mother that he could never forgive him for that and often upset my mother by referring to Roy as a coward.

I had been home for about four weeks now and still I hadn't seen Roy since he went into the army. What's more he hadn't seen my baby, and we had drifted apart from each other. We were both so busy trying to put together our mixed-up lives for nothing had gone right since we stepped off the ship coming back from Australia. I often wondered what would have happened to me had I stayed. At least all of us were treated the same over there, even if it was cruel sometimes, and I started to daydream again because nobody here cared about me I thought. There wasn't even Roy now and my stepfather always called me stupid or thick or he would say 'thick as two planks'. I hated him.

Being a mum soon brought me back to reality and I would pick up Heidi in my arms and say to her, 'You love me, don't you?' and then I would kiss her and say how much I loved her. Life was average, not wonderful, but routine. Then my world fell apart. My baby was now five weeks old, my mother and father had gone off to their places of work, and the younger children to school and the day started like any other day as I busied myself cleaning the house, washing clothes and taking care of my baby. There was a knock on the front door and I answered it to this middle-aged lady who stood there. 'Hello, my dear,' she said. 'Can I come in?' and with that she walked straight past me.

'Who are you?' I asked and she replied, 'Let's not take too much time, let's get it over with as quickly as possible, I always find it less painful that way.' She started to gather up things that belonged to Heidi and then asked to see the baby. She spotted her asleep in the chair and she picked her up and started to head for the front door saying, 'It's for the best, believe me, my dear, you'll see,' and off she went down the front path and got into a car that was waiting outside for her.

Everything happened so quickly: I can remember running after her screaming and yelling, 'Bring back my baby, help! She is stealing my baby.' The whole world seemed to be going around and round. I don't remember what happened next but I found myself in the next door neighbour's house and she was patting me on the back, asking me not to cry and saying, 'Drink your tea, it will make you feel better.'

'Nothing will make me feel better,' I snapped. 'I want my baby.' She had always been a good neighbour and she knew what it was like for Roy and me. Often she would talk to us over the fence and give us a big piece of bread pudding and say, 'Go on, off you go, before all the others want a piece.'

She was having a hard life herself at that time, having had two sons, and a husband who would come home on a Friday and give her housekeeping money, yet by morning he had stolen it back from her purse to spend on the horses. 'He is the generous sort,' she would say because if he won he would give her lots extra but if he lost, which was more often than not, she got nothing.

Still trying to calm me down she asked me who this lady was and why did she take my baby and swore that she knew nothing of all this. To this day I cannot believe that both my parents went off to work and had arranged for all this to take place without telling me or asking me, that they had arranged for Heidi 'my baby' to be adopted, but that's exactly what they did. I was to find out very soon that all that was left for me to do was sign the papers. There was a terrible silence at home that night it was as if everyone was afraid to ask or say anything. My stepfather ruled and, as always, everyone was afraid to question him, and that included my mother. His word was the last word and that is exactly what he said. 'We will put this matter to bed, here and now, and it will not be mentioned in this house again.'

I couldn't believe my ears. I hated him, oh how I hated him. How dare he, who was he that he could say and do this to me? I looked at my mother. 'Please,' I thought, 'please just for once say something to him,' but she didn't and said it would be best if I went and tidied my room. 'It's all for the best,' she said, just like that lady had said. As I walked up the stairs to my room, tears rolled down my face. I remember that I wanted to call out loud to someone to help me but there was no one to help, no one to care, and, after sobbing myself to sleep, I later woke to another day and life went on as though nothing had happened. Apart from a few whispered conversations at bedtime with my sisters and the signing of the adoption papers which had also been organised for me just like making out a shopping list, nobody ever spoke of my baby Heidi ever again.

A few weeks later Roy turned up at the front door. He had finished with his girlfriend and now had nowhere to live. I had managed to talk to him for a while in his room, all about the baby, and how I hated my stepfather, and I asked Roy why he ever wanted to come back here and he said he didn't want to but he had nowhere else to go. He didn't seem much interested in me and my troubles, having so many hang-ups of his own, for he had turned very moody and withdrawn. I knew that he too was searching for someone to love him and I remember we both sat there, much older now, and I held his hand like I always used to and said to him, 'Please don't be sad, Roy, don't worry, everything will be all right.' He looked at me and said, 'I'm supposed to say that to you,' so we both smiled and after brotherly and sisterly romps we picked ourselves up to face another day.

CHAPTER
SIX

It didn't take long for me to find work and I soon settled in working as a typist in a tobacco company and I really enjoyed it. I was now seventeen and a half and started to go out in the evenings after work and I had a girl friend, Maureen, who came from a lovely family. Her mother and father and her brother, John, really cared for her but sadly, soon after I met Maureen, her father died. Her mother was wonderful to me, so instead of going to see Maureen and go out with her, I would go and see her mother and stay in and just talk most of the time. I would say to her that I wished she was my mother, then I would feel so guilty for having such thoughts. She would buy me clothes, not very many, as times were hard for her since her husband had died. I remember on one occasion that she bought me a lovely, pink jumper. I had never seen anything like it in my whole life, let alone owned such a thing, and it was so wonderful I think I wore it every day until it wore away. I will always remember her kindness towards me in helping me through the many traumas that made up my life just by talking. Roy had got to know her also through me and quickly palled up with her son John and his group of friends, and we would all go to the local café and just sit and chat and play the latest records on the jukebox.

It was during one of those visits to the café that Roy introduced me to one of his friends with the nickname Deano. Roy had told me a lot about him and was always talking about him, said he was always at the café and always had money and cigarettes and was over from Ireland working here. I remember thinking to myself, where is Ireland? The way he dressed made him stand out in a crowd because he wore all the typical teddy-boy gear, white suit and white winkle-picker shoes with chains attached to them. At the time I wasn't sure it was him I was attracted to or all the attention he was getting. After a couple of meetings at the café he asked me out and I remember I was thrilled but I also knew that if my stepfather saw him he would go mad so I asked Roy to promise not to say anything at home. He did promise, but I always had my doubts that he would keep his promise because he had often lied before and got me into serious trouble, then would say to me that it was 'only a joke'.

I started seeing Deano nearly every night and I would give the excuse that I was going down my friend's house to do something, but then when our relationship became more serious I told my mother. She said that as I was nearly eighteen now I should have more sense and if I hadn't learnt my lesson by now I never would. She went on to say, 'Don't bring any more trouble home here.' I almost got excited that she hadn't stopped me seeing him and began to tell her all about him and when I began to describe how he dressed she said, 'You had better not bring him home here, or your father will have something to say.' I soon realised that my small burst of excitement had been in vain. I found out after a few months that Deano's real name was Denis but he had wanted to be called Deano after James Dean the film star who was all the rage in the cinemas then, or picture houses as they were called.

I started to get really involved with Denis and spent more and more of my time with him. He was staying in lodgings in town and I would go down after work and cook his tea for him and fuss over him. I was good at cooking and cleaning and I had certainly had enough practice I think most girls did in those days. I remember also pouring out all my darkest secrets to him and he would listen. On reflection I think it was only because he was tired and just glad to have someone to look after him after a hard day's work, turning his lonely lodgings into a cosy home. He would in turn tell me all about Ireland and his mother and one brother and how he would go back there one day, that he was only over here in England to work on the buildings to make some money, for work was short in Ireland at that time. I remember telling him about Heidi when we were in a picture house of all places and I took this little picture out of my purse. It was a picture of myself and Heidi taken by one of these passport machines just before she was taken from me and was all I had left of her except my memories. I handed it to him and like a little girl I said, 'Guess who?'

I think I was sort of asking him to help me get her back, and then we could all live happily ever after. In seconds, he jumped out of the seat and walked out and left me there but I chased after him as I always did and caught up with him outside but he said he didn't want to discuss it. Why would he want somebody else's child? He walked off again and still I ran after him and I asked for the photo back and said I was sorry. He turned to face me, handed me the photo and said, 'Tear it up, go on, tear it up and don't ever mention it again if you want me to stay with you.'

So that's what I did. I tore up this precious little photo and the tears rolled down my face; everything was horrible, I hated the whole world, but I loved Denis and would do anything to keep him. I often asked myself the question, did I know what love was? Nobody had ever loved me, so how would I know how to love? Looking back now, I think I would have loved anyone who showed any signs of affection.

It wasn't long before the next upheaval in my life was about to descend on me, Denis having decided to go back to Ireland. He had decided to go at the weekend and this was a Thursday that he was telling me and his very words to me were, 'You can come with me if you like, but if you don't it won't bother me.'

For a moment I felt hurt, but only for a moment because nothing he said or did wrong would upset me for long. I started to get all excited, jumping up and down. 'What, for good?' I asked. 'Leave here for good?'

'Yeah,' he said, 'if you want to.' Did I want to? Wow!

'I would love to,' and he too showed a bit of excitement.

'You will love my mother,' he said, 'and she will like you. She will probably wish I had met an Irish girl though,' he went on to say but I wasn't really listening. I was daydreaming again. Run away I thought, what an adventure, run away from all this with no parents to tell me what to do.

'How will we get there?' I asked.

'By ferry,' he said. 'But we will have a week in London first and I will show you all the good gear clothes shops.' It all sounded so wonderful, then I began to think how I would tell my parents. Would they let me go, I wondered? I remember working out a plan, although most of it was lies, but it was the only way. I used the same case that I had brought back from Australia, which had stayed under my bed all those years, full of odds and ends. I packed everything I owned, which wasn't a lot, and hid the suitcase behind the curtain that acted as a wardrobe in the bedroom. I had arranged to meet Denis at the bus depot at the top of the hill and had told him not to come anywhere near the house. I was so afraid that my stepfather was going to stop me and that he would ruin my chance. He had done that so many times in my life and I was determined not to let him this time.

I got up early on Saturday morning, trying not to make a sound, but my two sisters were awake. They were much older now, aged thirteen and fourteen and I had told them what I was doing. They too thought it was a great adventure and they said they would miss me but wished me luck. I walked out on the landing and my youngest brother came out of his room and said that Roy had told him I was leaving. I had told Roy a few days ago but I didn't think he really took much notice. He only seemed interested in this new girlfriend he had met. 'This is the one for me,' he would say. She was a nice girl, very young, but they seemed happy together. Roy had been living at her house for several weeks on and off and like me he would stay anywhere to get out of this house.

My youngest brother handed me a package. 'Here you are,' he said. It was ten cigarettes wrapped in toilet paper and as I opened it the tears welled up in my eyes. I loved my younger brother and two sisters very much and we were very close, even though my stepfather had tried all these years to keep us separate. However, the more he tried to keep us apart the closer we became. I didn't dare ask where he got the cigarettes from but I was so touched by his gift that's all that mattered to me. It's funny how some things really stand out in your mind, and this is one incident that does for me.

We all said goodbye to one another on the landing in a sort of whisper so as not to wake my stepfather next door. My mother was already up and I struggled down the stairs with the suitcase and heard her chopping sticks for the fire outside in the back yard. I walked up behind her and said, 'I'm going away with Denis for the weekend, Mum. He's taking me to meet some of his family living in London.' Of course I knew that it was longer than a weekend I was going for, but I thought it would be easier to write and tell her when I got there that I wouldn't be coming back at all. I remember my mother never turned around but for just a moment she stopped what she was doing and said, 'You make your bed, you lie on it, girl. I hope you've told your father.'

'No,' I said. 'I'll go and tell him now.' I went back in the house and as I got to the back door I said, 'Goodbye, Mum,' but there was no answer. I started to head for the stairs, terrified about how I was going to tell my father who might lock me in and might stop me from going. I tapped lightly on his bedroom door, 'Dad,' I called and looked around the door but he was in bed with his back to me. 'I'm going now. I'm going away with Denis for the weekend. I've told Mum, OK?' All I got was a grunt but I knew he had heard me and I didn't want to hang around any longer. I just wanted to get out and I hated him for not letting my mother love me; I would never forgive him for that.

It was seven-thirty on a Saturday morning and I was walking up the road with a huge suitcase praying with all my might that Denis would be at the depot to meet me. What if he wasn't there, what would I do? I could never go back home. In fact I wouldn't go back home and whilst I was thinking all this a neighbour asked me if he could help me with my suitcase and I was thrilled as it was getting heavier and heavier. He didn't ask any questions as I thought he might, but just chatted in general and before I knew it I was there at the bus depot. That's when a whole new episode of my life was about to begin. Denis was there and I remember thinking he must love me or he wouldn't have turned up. We hugged and I looked up at him and said, 'Guess what, I'm free.' But was I?

We caught the local bus to the bus station, then got a coach to London, Victoria, booking into a local bed and breakfast. I can remember feeling happy again. The last time I felt really happy had been when Heidi was born and I looked into her tiny little face. I always tried hard not to think of her, as I would get so upset and all the sadness and bitterness in my life would come flooding back. There were times when I just couldn't help thinking of her, especially when I was feeling happy, like now and I would begin to feel so guilty, and then it would all be spoilt.

What's New Pussycat, the new Peter Sellers film was showing at the local cinema in Victoria, and I remember we went to watch it and I felt so free, sometimes, it was quite scary, and I would half look around expecting to see my stepfather standing there. The whole week was hectic, mostly looking at all the clothes shops, and, before we knew it, we were heading for the docks at Holyhead to sail to Dublin. Sometimes I felt that one day I would find a place where I could belong, a place to settle, where I could be happy forever and ever. Perhaps it would be Ireland. Having lived with Denis for a whole week, I began to see that he had a very bad temper and I discovered he was a very jealous person too. When I tried to make myself pretty for him, he would accuse me of doing it for someone else even though there wasn't anyone else around. He would get angry with anyone passing who looked at me and he would then accuse me of encouraging them. I tried hard not to take any notice of him and thought if I ignored all the moods and abuse it would go away. But sometimes it didn't work and he would push me or threaten me, then walk off. Always I would chase after him because I loved him, I kept telling myself, I loved him.

On the ferry, we spent most of our time on the slot machines, as that's what he liked to do, and he would lose vast amounts of money, and, the more he lost, the angrier he would get. As long as I kept silent things would be right, but if I said anything, and I remember one instance when I said, 'Oh, come on, Denis, this is for losers,' his whole personality would change almost like Jekyll and Hyde. He would kick the machine, tell me to get lost and say really hurtful things to me like 'who needs you anyway?' and then he would start telling me all about an Irish girl whom he loved, that one day he would go back to her. I would often end up in tears, and pray that he would say sorry and make a fuss of me, but he never did—or at least not until the next day, after I had cried all night, and been left on my own in the cabin, feeling sad, lonely and afraid. I would always forgive him, always say sorry to him, throw my arms around him and say, 'I love you.'

Arriving at Dun Laoghaire, approximately three miles outside Dublin, we were able to catch a bus to Dublin with another five-minute bus ride to his mother's place. We were happy again now he had come home because he was very proud of his country, very proud to be Irish. On the bus journey, I had showered him with questions about his home and his mother and brother. 'Will they like me?' was my main question, and in my mind I prayed that they would, not daring to think about what would happen if they didn't. We got off the bus and there was a short walk up a steep hill and just around the corner at the top of the hill was where his family lived. It was a block of flats and there were rows and rows of these flats. I had never seen anything like this before, and I remember thinking how nice that everyone lived so close to each other.

Worn out from carrying our luggage—and I always had to do my share—we arrived at the second block. 'Just up one flight of stairs,' he said. 'Second balcony, and that's where Ma lives and Sean, my kid brother.' I felt my stomach turn and I tried to straighten my hair, having been brought up to believe that first impressions were very important. 'Come on,' he said, 'you look great.' Those few words gave me confidence and as he knocked on the door I stood there feeling a little bit more relaxed. A fair-haired lady came to the door wearing a warm and welcoming smile, and she threw her arms around her son, then said, 'And so, this is Susan. I have heard so much about you; come on in and get warm by the fire.' And Denis looked back at me and said so proudly, 'I told you, I told you she would like you.'

'Where's Sean?' he said and his mother said that his younger brother was at work and would be home shortly, and she went on to say how pleased he would be to see us both.

After making us a cup of tea, and pushing the armchairs nearly into the fire so we could be nice and warm there was a knock on the door and his mother answered it, and came back in to the living room, followed by two policemen. Denis jumped up. 'What's going on?' he said, very quickly on the defensive. They explained that he had to go with them to the station because he had been in trouble before he left for England and they wanted to sort things out. They had heard that he had stepped foot back in Dublin and they wanted to talk with him down at the station. I remember his mother was very much in his defence, saying, 'How dare they, and he only just put his foot in the door,' but nothing she said would deter them. Denis went with them but as he left the doorway he looked back at his mother and said, 'Don't worry, Ma,' and then he was gone.

I sat there feeling very nervous. How many times had I heard that expression in my life—'Don't worry'? His mother was more than kind to me; she was wonderful and she made me feel so welcome, although a couple of times she intimated that she would have liked her son to meet a nice Irish girl. Yet she said it in a way not be to taken offensively. She waited on me hand and foot, and couldn't do enough to help me, asking me about my parents and how good they were, she said, to let you come and stay. I didn't dare tell her the truth and obviously her son hadn't, and I certainly didn't want to be the cause of any upsets between them. It did remind me, though, that I would have to write to my parents and explain that I was settled and happy and tell them no to worry. That was a joke, 'worry' about me, but it was nice to think sometimes that they might!

Sean came home from work. He was just seventeen but he didn't resemble his brother in looks. He was fairer and had a rounder face, and he had a smile and a personality that would light up a whole room of people. 'Hi there,' he said, and came over and shook hands with me. 'I'm Sean and you must be Susan. What's for tea, Ma, I'm starving?' And that was Sean. I found out later that everyone loved Sean. He would do anything for anyone, any time and he was always happy, even when there was nothing to be happy about. I could see he adored his mother. Denis also loved his mother, but in a more reserved way. Sean was jolly, always joking with her, praising her. Denis was more moody and she would often say to me that he was difficult to approach but he was the more sensible one. She went on to say that when their father died whilst he and Sean were only three and five years of age, Denis had been made to promise that he would be the man of the house and look after his mother and younger brother. I remember feeling what a terrible burden to put on such a small child and I started to feel guilty about feeling so awful about my own childhood.

Later that evening Denis came back home, and when his mother and I asked him what it was all about, he said, 'Nothing, they had heard I was back in the country and wanted to give me a few warnings.' We both felt that there was more to it than that, but didn't challenge him any further. In fact, I soon began to notice that his mother reacted very much like I did towards him. We would just smooth things over so as not to upset him.

His mother took to me like a daughter. It was marvellous. We shopped together, did the housework together, when she would let me, and often she would spoil me and let me sit by the fire whilst she cleaned the flat or cooked something nice for tea. There was never a lot of money to go round but what there was she certainly made go round but as the weeks turned into months

I saw less and less of Denis. He had bought himself a motorbike and was always out with his mates. He was quite happy to leave me as company to his mother, and I was happy for him to do so. I was now like a sister to Sean and he would bring home his friends and we would play cards for pennies, sometimes playing all night, and end up going to bed when the milkman was arriving at six-thirty the next morning. Looking back now, I was happy that Denis wasn't there very often because when he wasn't there everything was happy and fun and when he was there always seemed to be aggravation. I know, now, that I was very afraid of him, very afraid of his moods and how he would react to them. His mother also knew this but always chose to change the subject if I discussed it with her or she would say, 'He loves you really, he doesn't mean it,' and I believed her.

For a few weeks now I had been scouring the papers looking at all the adverts to get a job. I knew I was good at shorthand and typing but I was not familiar with my new surroundings and I didn't know my way about very well so I would shout out as I was reading, where is this and where is that. With the help of Ma, as I now called her, although it took me a long time to get used to calling her Ma, we decided to write to a few chosen job ads. Whilst I was writing the letters she asked me had I written to my parents yet? Yes I had, I replied, several weeks ago. I also think she could see I was disappointed that I hadn't had a reply yet and she got back on the subject of writing for the jobs. It wasn't long before I got a reply from a local company who had advertised for an accounting machine operator, saying thank you for my letter, and would I be able to attend for an interview? I was jumping up and down with excitement and I remember Sean mucking about and saying he would bet me ten fags that I would get the job. The fact that he bet me that I would get the job and not that I wouldn't get it made me feel great.

I did get it. I think they were quite fascinated that I was an English girl and they said they liked my accent but they were very friendly, it being a family business with garage and car showrooms. Start Monday they said, salary £4.4s.0d per week, which was about average then, and I was over the moon. I couldn't believe all this happiness and good luck was happening to me. It turned out to be the kind of job that I wanted to be doing twenty-four hours a day; they were wonderful to me and I loved every bit of it. One of the directors treated me like a daughter and I would sometimes look after the youngest of his seven children. I worked in the office upstairs with a lady far senior to me, and I have so much to thank her for because she taught me so much. Miss Hanrahan, I will always remember her. She gave me my first fountain pen, which I still have to this day. Although she could be strict at times she would say in a kind voice afterwards, 'It's all for your own good, Susan, you'll thank me one day,' and I do, most sincerely. The other director's daughter would work in the reception area and her fiancé worked along side her. We were all very friendly and helpful to each other and all worked well as a team. I got to know most of the mechanics working in the garage and they were all very friendly. At lunchtimes, we would play handball up against the garage door. I loved anything sporty and I remember when I was a child in Australia I was in the school netball team and I was second in the long jump. An Aborigine girl could jump fourteen foot eight inches and I could jump thirteen foot ten inches and we used to tour all the other local schools competing for the trophies.

Whilst I was working for the motor car company I met a girl called Flo and we got on so well together we soon became very good friends. I met her family who lived on the other side of Dublin and I took her to meet Denis and his family. He wasn't very enamoured by this turn of events, not because of Flo, but because I had met a friend and we were seeing quite a lot of each other. I recall on one particular night she asked me to go to the theatre with her because there was a live show, telling me it was good fun and that she had been to one before. There was going to be a hypnotist there, she said, and he would invite people in the audience to participate, then hypnotise them and make them do funny things. After much thought I said yes, yes I would go with her, although I knew telling Denis wasn't going to be easy with his fiery temper and his jealousy but, on my way home from work, I practised over and over what I would say to him. I wouldn't tell a lie but I would play it down so he wouldn't think that I was going to enjoy myself and that way I thought everything would be all right.

I was home from work first that evening and, as usual, his mother had my tea ready; she was so good to me. Then Sean came in from work and I started to tell them both that I was going to tell Denis when he came in that I was going out with Flo that night to a show. I was more or less asking them both how they thought he would react. His mother seemed to turn pale. 'Oh Susan,' she said, 'do you think you should? You know how upset he gets,' and she went on and on, trying everything in her power to get me to change my mind. Sean just said that I should be able to do anything I liked; why did I have to ask? And with that he got up, lit a cigarette and said, 'I'm off out now, Ma. I won't be late, bye,' and he looked at me on the way out and said, 'Have a nice time. It will do you good to enjoy yourself,' and then he was gone.

I had arranged to meet Flo in town so that meant that I would have to get the bus at the bottom of the hill. I looked at the time but Denis wasn't home yet so I thought I would have to get ready first, then tell him. I went into the bedroom and his mother followed me once again saying, 'Oh please, Susan, don't go,' but I told her everything would be all right and not to worry. For a moment, after saying those words, my memory went back to Roy, and I wondered how he was. Where was he? And why had I not had a letter from my mother yet? I had been gone almost three months now and admittedly I had only written two letters but that was because I was waiting for a reply. My thoughts came back to the present when I heard Denis walk through the door, and his mother went to the kitchen to get his tea and make herself busy. I could see she was getting really nervous, and I didn't want to hurt her, as she was so good to me.

'Where are you off to then?' he asked.

73

'I'm going to a show with Flo,' I said. 'It's on in town so I won't be late.' I could feel myself stuttering and tried to carry on getting ready whilst I was talking.

'Oh yeah, what bloody show?' he asked and I started to get nervous, not wanting any trouble.

I tried to explain that it wasn't much, it was just that I had promised my friend that I would go with her.

He went into the living room mumbling, and then said, 'I'm going out anyway. Do as you bloody well like, I don't care.'

His mother came out of the kitchen carrying his tea. 'Here you are, son,' she said. 'Get that down you, it'll do you good,' and she was fussing all over him, trying to keep him calm. He didn't say anything else; he just sat and ate his tea, and I stayed in the bedroom to finish getting ready. I didn't dress up; I was too scared to dress up in fancy clothes, so I chose something that made me look drab. Then I looked at the time again and hovered in the bedroom, too scared to come out. At last, I heard him get up and say, 'I'm off now, Ma. Don't wait up for me.' The front door slammed and he was gone. His mother came into me all flustered and said one more time, 'Please don't go,' but I was determined. He had gone out—he went out every night—but I never asked any questions and he hardly ever took me out. In fact I didn't even feel like his girlfriend, more like a companion to his mother. I went out the front door and I saw him disappear around the corner on his motor bike and just for a moment I thought he might wait for me at the bottom of the hill. I once again looked at the time and found I needed to rush for the bus, so I said goodbye to this mother, told her not to worry, that I would be home before him. I walked down the hill to the bus stop, looking back every so often to see her waving to me from the balcony.

Both Flo and I had the time of our lives that evening—nothing improper—we sat in our seats, which were similar to those in a cinema and watched the show. It was hilarious. I never laughed so much in all my life as we tried to push each other up to be volunteers on the stage but neither of us succeeded although I remember the hypnotist changed a group of young lads into leprechauns. They were running in and out of the audience in their delusion; others were chickens, and he changed boys into girls and girls into boys and the whole show was just good clean fun. We found ourselves outside, still laughing, and going back over the show repeatedly with each other when I asked her the time. 'Eleven o'clock,' she said.

I suddenly felt sick with fear because I had missed my last bus; the last bus was at eleven, and I knew I could walk. It wasn't too far, but it would take me longer and I wanted to get home before he did. I said goodbye to Flo in a hurry and shouted as I ran, 'See you at work in the morning.'

I ran as fast as I could and I could feel my heart thumping in my chest but I wasn't sure whether it was from running or feeling scared. I got to the bottom of the hill, took a deep breath, and ran up it. Heading round the corner, I looked up towards the flat but this didn't tell me anything. The lights were always on anyway and I knew his mother would be waiting up for me, even if he wasn't in. It was just after eleven-thirty when I ran up the steps to the second balcony, and put my key in the door. Before I could turn it, the door opened and Denis stood there. 'Where the bloody hell have you been?' and with that he head-butted me right in the face and, as I screamed, he dragged me in to the hallway and slammed the door.

Blood was pouring out of my nose and his mother was standing beside me in seconds of him doing it. 'Oh my God,' she said. 'What have you done?'

I could hear him: 'I'm so sorry, I didn't mean to, oh God, I'm so sorry.'

His mother replied, 'She'll have to go to hospital and have stitches,' and by this time she had given me a towel from the bathroom to cover my face.

'She is not going to hospital,' he roared. 'No way, do you hear me?' And he barricaded the front door.

'All right,' his mother said. 'Calm down,' and she took me into the living room, sat me down, and said, 'Let me have a look.' As I took the towel away, she said she would bathe it. As she was bathing my nose, she kept saying, 'He didn't mean it, he loves you really, he didn't mean it.' But I was too scared to say anything and I could see him sitting at the table with his head in his hands, mumbling to himself and then he asked where Sean was. 'He's not home yet,' his mother said, and I could see her mind working because she knew that when Sean came in and found out what he had done to me they would both end up fighting and that was every mother's nightmare, two sons fighting each other.

Denis then looked up at me and said, 'You fell up the concrete steps outside on your way up tonight OK? And if you say otherwise I'll kill you.'

'You'll do nothing of the sort,' his mother said. 'You've half killed her now. What is the matter with you?'

He started to get angrier and tipped the chairs over and then shouted for us both to keep our bloody mouths shut or he would shut them for us. Then walked out of the living room into his bedroom, looking back and saying 'You fell up the bloody stairs, don't you forget that, and no bloody hospital.' With that, he went into his bedroom and slammed the door shut. His mother did the best she could with my nose, for it was already swelling fast, and she said for me to go to bed before Sean came in as she was afraid there would be trouble.

I went to bed that night feeling like I had gone ten rounds with a boxer but, more than that, I lay in bed saying over and over to myself, 'I hate him, I hate him.' My memory went back to my stepfather and to the house-masters of the children's home, then I started to say that I hated all men, every last one of them. Then I felt guilty, because I didn't hate Roy. I loved Roy and I wished he was here now to hold my hand and say, 'Don't worry, I'll look after you.' I lay awake for hours, planning how I would escape in the morning, how I would run away. I would tell his mother and Sean because they were so good to me but I would have to run away from him. Where would I go? I couldn't go home. I had nowhere to go, and I thought of my job; they were good to me, maybe they would help, but how could I let them see me like this? I would have to ring in and say I wasn't well. I put the sheets over my sore face and eventually sobbed myself to sleep.

I awoke the next morning early and, feeling very sore, I got up to go to the bathroom. At first I was too scared to look in the mirror, but I plucked up the courage and what I saw was horrible. My nose was very swollen, my eyes were very bruised and there was a big gash on the bridge of my nose with congealed blood stuck to it. I started to cry and went into the kitchen to make a cup of tea when his mother came out and asked me how I was, still saying that he didn't mean it and that I should have never gone out and it wouldn't have happened. 'But I didn't do anything wrong,' I said. 'I only went to a show with my friend; he can't keep me a prisoner, Anyway, I have decided to go home.'

I don't know where these words came from—they just seemed to come out like that—but his mother turned a little angry. 'You can't go home; I'm responsible for you and unless your mother comes and gets you, you'll stay here,' she said.

I started to laugh, my face hurting all the more. 'You're joking,' I replied. 'My mother come and fetch me? That's a laugh; she doesn't even care about me,' and the tears were rolling down my face.

She hugged me and tried to comfort me, and said that in a few days it would all be over and I would feel different, that I could go back to work, and everything would go back to normal.

'What about the next time?' I asked.

'There won't be a next time, I'll make sure of that,' she said. Then we sat and drank a nice cup of tea and I stuck to the story of falling up the stairs and everyone felt sorry for me. Later I went to the hospital and told them the same thing. Because Denis was with me I couldn't say otherwise, and they said I would always have a scar as I should have come to the hospital as soon as it happened. They put five stitches in but I don't remember feeling any pain but I think I was too scared to feel anything.

I told everyone at work the same story and, like his mother said, the whole episode came and went like it had never happened and I got on with my life, holding my breath, waiting, always waiting, for the next time. I couldn't feel close to him any more after that but I was also too scared to leave him. He continued to go out most nights on his own and I stayed in with his mother or Sean and his friends. Then one night I got brave and I decided to follow him out to see what he got up to. His mother was going frantic. 'You're asking for trouble,' she told me. 'If he finds out he'll kill you,' but I went anyway.

I left about an hour after he did, just to make sure the coast was clear. I caught the bus at the bottom of the hill into town, as it was only a couple of stops and a straight road. I had just got off of the bus, now feeling that I wished I hadn't, when a voice said, 'Hello Sue, what are you doing here?' I looked around and it was Denis' best friend, Noel, and I told him that I had come looking for Denis. He said, 'He's over there in the café, but don't go over there, you're a nice girl. Go on, go back home.'

I did go home, not having the courage to go and walk in the café and I would have been too scared to say anything if I had. I will always remember his friend, Noel, for his kind words to me and I remember it wasn't long after that that he was killed in a stabbing. He had gone to assist another young lad and the assailant had turned on him and stabbed him to death. He left a young wife and two young children.

I didn't go out with Flo any more after that but she did start coming around the house more often and after a while I began to realise why. Flo and Sean had begun to really like each other and started to see each other often. In fact they soon became inseparable. I was pleased for both of them. I loved Sean, as a brother, and Flo was my best friend so what better combination could there be?

CHAPTER
SEVEN

It was soon big news in Dublin that President John F Kennedy was coming to Ireland and on his visit to Dublin he would stay at Phoenix Park where the President of Southern Ireland resided. That meant that he would be passing right by the bottom of the little hill where we lived. To see the President of the United states of America was one of the most outstanding moments in my life and as I stood at the bottom of the hill that day and he drove past, in an open topped saloon car, he stood up in the car waving to the crowds. He was wearing a light blue suit and he was fabulously sun-tanned, his smile revealing a set of teeth that were just like pearls. I could have reached out and touched him, I was so close, and it was a fantastic moment for me and, I am sure, for many others. It was a day that will stay with me forever, especially after his tragic death, later, in America.

Arriving home from work one day—just like any other day— there was a letter from my mother and I didn't even wait to take off my shoes or my coat. I tore it open and it was written quite formally. My mother hoped I was well and said the youngsters sent their love but mostly the letter was about Roy. He was about to be married, to Jean who was the same girl he was with when I left England and they were to be married very soon, as Jean was expecting a baby and I was invited to the wedding. I remember jumping up and down, singing and dancing around the room, and I think it was because I could be going home! Although all these years I had hated home and been so unhappy,

I always hoped with all my heart that this would change and somehow, someday, a fairy would have a magic wand and I would be in the happiest home in the whole world. I was twenty years of age now and still I was day-dreaming. I answered my mother's letter immediately because I wanted to make sure that the invitation was for both Denis and I. See how soon I had forgotten all the fear I had for him!

Within a week, because of the early wedding date, I'm sure, I had a reply to my letter but mother said sorry, the invitation was for me only. My stepfather would pay my fare to fly over, which was seven pounds and ten shillings. I didn't know what to say to Denis. I could only think that he would become angry again, so I decided to tell him that if he couldn't go, then I wouldn't either. To my amazement he said he didn't want to go anyway and that I could do what I liked.

I remember I borrowed the fare from my job and said I would pay it back when I returned as I was only going for the weekend. It was only an hour's flight but I had never flown before so I was very nervous. Denis didn't take me to the airport; he wasn't in the mood, he said, so one of the lads from work took me. When I arrived back in England I made my own way to the house because the journey wasn't long and I didn't want anyone to think that I couldn't manage. In fact, I wanted to show off. I wanted everyone to say, 'Oh, she's done well for herself,' but I don't suppose they did, although I felt very grown up and independent. When I got to the house it was all hugs and kisses. My two 'baby' sisters were no longer babies—they were fourteen and fifteen, and my young brother was sixteen. We were so pleased to see each other again and I was so pleased to see my mother except she seemed different—more relaxed. Maybe that's because I had been away; she was never a person to show her emotions, perhaps because of her sad childhood.

She did say how smart I looked and asked me all about how I was getting on, although I pretended a lot, being too proud to say that my relationship with my boyfriend was awful and that he was violent. I felt she might have said, 'Well what do you expect? All men are violent,' so I said I was really happy, I told her how lovely his mother was. That wasn't a lie; I loved her very much and she was so kind to me. My mother seemed pleased and she said she was glad that I had settled down and then went on to say that it would be a good thing if I went to say thank you to my father for the money for the trip. I said I would later, but right now I wanted to see Roy. He was out she said and would be back soon—last-minute things for the big day tomorrow she had said. I wanted her to say to me how happy she was that Roy had met a nice girl and was getting married because I knew this would make my mother happy. Deep down inside, I felt that she wanted us both to turn out really well so she could say something to my stepfather, but as always she said very little. Would she ever say she loved us, I asked myself?

Roy came through the door and I ran to him and hugged him. He was so grown up but we were like strangers now and I felt he had gone on with his life while I had dwelt on the past too much in mine. I always wanted to know the answer to everything. Why was I in a home? Why was I sent to Australia? Why didn't anyone love me? Why, why, why...? and then tears would fill up in my eyes and I would have to try and hide them, but this was not the time for tears. This was a wedding celebration, my brother's wedding, and I was so very happy for him.

Sadly, as always, all good things come to an end. The wedding had gone well; it was now Sunday and I had to be back at the airport to catch the plane. It only seemed like only minutes ago that I was saying all my hellos and now it was goodbyes but I thanked my stepfather for the money and wished that I could have said, 'No thank you, I have my own money.' Yet I didn't and I, whatever he had done in the past, was grateful that he had made it possible for me to go to Roy's wedding.

Back in Dublin, with all the celebrations behind me, there was plenty to talk about. Denis' mum wanted to hear everything, saying she loved weddings and I don't think she ever believed that I was really that unhappy at home. I think she thought it was just childish stories on my part.

By this time Seán and Flo had become very close and there was talk that they were going to go to England to look for work. The construction industry had been on strike now, in Dublin, for nearly thirteen weeks and Denis was getting really unsettled, and he and Sean had been talking about making big money in England. His mother was very upset. To lose one of her sons was hard, but both of them was tragic, especially as she and Sean got on so well.

There seemed to be no early let-up to the strike, and day after day Denis got more and more irritable because he always liked to have money in his pocket for a rainy day and his reserves were dwindling fast. Then, after nearly fourteen weeks, he could stand no more and one evening announced that he was going back to England and told me to tell my job that I would be leaving at the coming weekend. I was dumbstruck; I couldn't believe it. How could I tell my employers? How could I leave here? His mother, his brother and my friends at work—all the happiness I had ever known was here. He could go, I thought, and I will stay but, as always, I didn't have the courage to say this. The next day I went into work and I told them what had happened. They knew my relationship with Denis was violent and they knew that I was afraid of him and they offered me a flat nearby and to help me out until I could stand on my own two feet. They did everything they could to persuade me to stay but I was too afraid. However, I promised them one thing. I promised them that I would give one month's notice and that under no circumstances would I leave that weekend; they had been so good towards me so that was the very least I could do for them.

I went home that evening scared out of my wits but determined to tell him that I would follow him back to England in one month, and, as always, I told his mother first. I don't really know how she felt; she wanted me to be with her but she also wanted me to be with her son because, she said, I always kept him on the straight and narrow. That was a joke really, since he kept himself exactly where he wanted to be kept—it was nothing to do with me. He was his own man at all times. I did tell him that evening, busying myself to distance myself from the subject and he looked up and said, 'Good, you can sell the car; and that will give me time to get somewhere sorted out to live.'

Live, I thought, does that mean for me too? Because, although I had written several letters to my parents in the three years I had been in Dublin, I had had only one or two replies. One of them had been when Roy had married and the other, ironically, was when my eldest brother, Alan, had got married. I hadn't been invited, not expecting my stepfather to pay out for me again, and, reading my mother's letter, it hadn't been very pleasant for her either. Apparently Alan had sent an open invitation to the house and being my mother's first-born (and I am sure to this day that she also adored Alan, but was never allowed to show it), she wanted to go to the wedding. My stepfather had read the guest list and found out that her first husband, my real father, was to be there with his new wife and two sons. He had flatly refused to go and said that my mother was not going either; apparently, on this occasion, she disobeyed his wishes and said she was going. Whilst at the church, feeling proud of her son, as I am sure she was, my stepfather turned up, drunk and unshaven and shouting abuse, and she went on to say in her letter that she was so upset that she left early. Roy had been there and had spoken briefly to his real father, probably as I would have, just to invoke some sort of recognition but there was little response and he has since passed away. She had ended the letter by saying that it was only natural for my stepfather to have behaved in this way and although it wasn't written there, her letter it more or less implied that she was wrong to have gone, and, if she hadn't, there would have been no trouble. The letter ended with, 'Take care, Susan, love Mum.' It was after I received that letter from my mother that I began to realise how very much we were alike and that, like me, she wanted to pour her heart out to someone.

I hoped with all my heart that Denis would include me when he had found somewhere to live in England because I didn't feel that I could go back home and I never considered that living with him might be worse. I never seemed to make my own decisions—I was always swept along with the tide. For instance, I would have loved with all my heart to stay where I was, to have taken that little flat, kept my job, and started a whole new independent life but I was too scared. I was not scared of the challenge; I could face that all right. I was scared that he would come looking for me and that there would be trouble. Nowadays, I can't believe how scared I was of him. I thought I loved him; I wanted to love him, and I wanted him to love me.

That weekend came and he left. I went to the railway station with him and waved him off and I always remember how he left me stranded there with no money to get home. I didn't seem to mind, I wouldn't have dared ask him for money, I would only get shouted at with a 'what have you done with your own money?' and I wouldn't dare say that I had spent most of it on him—cigarettes, presents, trying to buy his love. I walked home for living in a big city makes every journey a short one, and I enjoyed the freedom knowing that after a few hours he wouldn't be in the country. That made me feel sort of safe, although, when I had thoughts like this I would feel guilty and tell myself I loved him and in a strange sort of way I did.

When I got back to the house Sean was there and when he found out that I had walked home he went mad, calling his brother all the names under the sun, and said to me, 'I don't know why you stay with him.' I replied, without thinking, 'Because I love him.'

His mother was upset that he had gone back to England. Being very patriotic, like most of the Irish, she said she didn't know what England had to offer that Ireland didn't. She was hoping to save Sean from going but all her words of persuasion were in vain for he and Flo had decided to go a few weeks after me; I don't know why but they decided to go to London. I think Sean wanted to be independent of his brother and make it on his own, so he could feel proud. There was a lot of Irish coming over to England for work in those days and England was looked upon by some as the land of opportunity although they never lost their patriotism and returned home to see their families whenever possible. I had spoken several times on the phone with Denis, having promised him when he went that I would ring him when he got settled. He had rung the corner shop that his mother used, leaving a message and number for me to ring, saying he had found lodgings but no females were allowed and he went on to say that he couldn't wait for me to arrive, that he missed me. I told him that I had sold the car for fifty pounds and that I would bring the money with me. That was a lot of money then, and I thought he would be pleased with my efforts but he didn't say much.

My last day at work was sad. I really loved these people and I had become very good at my job thanks to Miss Hanrahan from whom I had learnt so much about book-keeping and accounting. I could now run the office on my own, which I often did when she was on sick leave or holiday. Everyone came into the office to wish me well for my return to England. They asked me to keep in touch and I promised I would and that I would never forget them, especially for their kindness towards me. I said my goodbyes that day with tears in my eyes, and asked myself why was it that I was always leaving one place to go to another.

Two days later I also said goodbye to 'Ma', Sean and Flo. I told them how much I would miss them and promised that I would write. I always remember how hard it must have been for Denis' mother who had lost first, Denis to England, now me, and in a few weeks Sean and Flo would be on their way. With all her family gone away, how lonely she would be, I thought.

A few hours later I was back in England and Denis met me from the airport, having taken time off work to do so. This made me feel wanted, helping to make some of my fears go away, at least for the time being. He had bought an old car to get himself back and forth to work and I remember as he drove me to his new lodging place that I felt a little excited at the thought of yet another new adventure. I asked him if his landlady had changed her mind and decided to let me stay but he said, 'You will have to go to your parents, but you can come and visit me any time you like.' I remember starting to cry because I didn't want to have to ask my parents if I could come home. I was twenty-one now, and the thought of going there and saying, 'Can I come home, please,' gave me the shivers.

I could never remember any really happy times at home, or memories that would draw me back there, except, of course, for thoughts of my two younger sisters and young brother. It would be wonderful to see them again, I thought, but how would I ask my parents? That would be the worst, knowing my stepfather would be as sarcastic as he always had been in the past. Denis' lodging place was very basic—one room with a shared bathroom—and he introduced me to his landlady who was a friendly middle-aged lady but also firm in her manner. After we had said hello to each other, she emphasised the fact that she would have no 'girls' staying in her house. I could come and visit at any time but would have to be gone by ten-thirty in the evening. I remember thinking here I was now aged twenty-one and still people were telling me what to do. A few minutes later I had climbed a flight of stairs to Denis' room and had forgotten all about the landlady and her rules. The room was cosy, although not very well furnished, but warm and clean. I set about making a cup of tea and I chatted on about leaving my job and his mother and brother, and how they had sent their love and how Sean and Flo would be in London in a few weeks time, and that we could go and visit them. He never showed any excitement about my suggestions but he did say that he was pleased that I was now here with him and promised me that everything would be all right.

Early that evening, he took me to my parents' house, which was only a few miles from where he was staying, and I remember sitting in the car outside pleading with him to come in with me. After all, I had been with him now for just over three years and they had seen him once or twice but never actually met him. His sense of dress had been toned down slightly—not a lot, but enough to help gain the acceptance of my parents. Eventually he agreed to come in with me and although he thought it best that I do this on my own he relented in my favour. I knocked on the door and my stepfather answered. The greeting was, 'Oh my God, what do you want?'

'Hello, Dad,' I said, still afraid of him, which induced in me in a sense of respect for him. As I said hello, I walked in, holding Denis' hand, dragging him with me. The look on my mother's face was at first, I thought, one of pleasure, but it was quickly replaced by shock. I introduced Denis to the family, acting bravely, but I didn't feel brave. My younger brother and sisters were more grown up now and it didn't take me long to find out how lenient my stepfather was with them, much more so than he had been with Roy and me. Surprisingly, I never ever felt jealous of them. I think that's because I loved them so much and I remember thinking how he had tried so hard all those years to separate us only to succeed in bringing us closer together. For this I could thank him.

The first few minutes following Denis' introduction to my parents were a little strained, but soon enough everything seemed to go quite smoothly. I do remember on one occasion my stepfather inviting Denis to stay for the weekend, and giving me instructions to make a bed up for him in the front room. In the front room I thought! Nobody was ever allowed to use the front room so I whispered to him how privileged he was. Of course there were strict orders from my stepfather for me not to do any sleep-walking, and he said if I chose to disobey him I would know what for. I wanted to remind him I was twenty-one now but I didn't dare.

CHAPTER
EIGHT

The days and months went by with little change and I managed to get work very quickly. I remember I was criticised because I took a job in a shoe factory where the wages were very good and I was on piece work and could earn three times what I could get in an office. I remember my stepfather saying that all factory girls were 'common trollops' but I also remember my mother being glad of the extra money I could bring home, and I think between them they decided to leave things as they were.

I would visit Denis most nights and I would often get there before he got home from work and would have his tea waiting for him, and I did his washing and cleaning and generally looked after him. I also kept in touch by letter to his mother and he was grateful for that because like most men he didn't like letter-writing. I also wrote a few letters to the company where I worked whilst living in Dublin, but gradually the letters dwindled off to a card at Christmas, although I always kept in touch.

Sean and Flo had moved to London and we also wrote to each other. Not many of us had the luxury of a telephone in the house in those days so our only contact was by letter. They were doing fine, struggling they had said, but then most of us were and they announced that they were to be married soon. Flo was expecting a baby and would we accept their invitation to the wedding, which we did, and for me especially it was lovely to see them again. They were so happy together and they had rented a flat, Sean managing to get work with a construction company, and working overtime to save more money for their new addition to the family.

Back home things weren't too wonderful and I didn't get on very well with my mother, clashing a lot. To me it seemed that she was jealous of my young age as if her life had passed her by.

She had had three children, then remarried, had another three and with all the sadness in between, I think I can understand now how she felt. At that time I didn't understand, and I would rebel, always saying to her how I knew she loved Roy more than she loved me, and she would respond by saying, 'Well, would you wonder why?' And sometimes she would say in an argument, 'You're no daughter of mine,' and I would shout back, 'Well, whose am I then?'

Everything seemed very strained at home and on some occasions I was asked to look after the younger ones. They would hate it as they were very grown up for their age and they would call me bossy boots, then there would be another argument, and I would always be blamed. I always felt like the Cinderella of the family, ever since I had come back from Australia, all those years ago. There had been nothing but arguments in the family and I often wondered where I would be now and what I would be doing if I had stayed in Australia.

Roy's marriage wasn't going too well. With Jean being very young when they got married—just sixteen and pregnant—it wasn't a very good recipe for starting a marriage. They had two children by now, but I didn't see either of them very often now as they lived quite a distance away from us.

Life continued to go on as normal, Denis and I having ups and downs like most, with him working seven days a week; the more money he could earn, the more he could save. I must admit he worked really hard and deserved every penny he earned but I could never fathom out why he wanted to save so much. I would often suggest he helped Sean and Flo out as by now they had had a baby girl, and were really struggling to keep their heads above water but he always declined. Then I would suggest he sent his mother some extra money or something nice. After all, I would say, she was so good to us. But he would never part with more than he had to. I never blamed him for this because he had worked hard for his money and it was his to do with as he wished.

Then another bombshell hit me, I was pregnant. I had had a feeling for several weeks but had been trying hard not to think about it. I had been with Denis for nearly five years now although the relationship wasn't very stable and we often had massive arguments, especially if I ever mentioned getting married, and settling down. He would always say that he wasn't the marrying kind and if I wanted to go then 'feel free' but how was I going to tell him that I was going to have his baby? And although I was nearly twenty-three now, how on earth was I going to tell my parents?

I decided to wait until the weekend to tell Denis. So I had booked with a local coach company to go to Bournemouth for a day at the seaside, thinking that would be a good time to break the news to him.

Saturday came and Denis was in a good mood, this being the first day off work he had had for some time. The sun was shining and he told me he was looking forward to lying on the beach, getting a sun-tan and just relaxing for the day. Although I tried to join in with his enthusiasm, my thoughts revolved around the secret I was about to unburden.

After a lovely day we were on our way back to the coach for our journey home and I still hadn't told him. I remember getting back to the coach park and standing around waiting for all the other passengers to arrive. It was then that I turned to him and said, 'Denis, I have something important to tell you.'

Half-interested and tired from the day's outing he answered, 'Well what is it?'

And scared out of my wits I told him that I was nearly three months' pregnant. I remember his face to this day just staring in shock, then like a roar of thunder out came a tirade. 'Get rid of it, I don't want a kid! I have always told you I don't want to get married, and how do I know it's mine?'

It seemed to go on and on while I just stood there shaking, too frightened to say anything. Then, without warning, I found myself bent over in terrible pain, tears coming from my eyes while I heard him say. 'There, that should get rid of it.' He had punched me so hard in the stomach that I felt that I had been hit by a car. Within seconds of all this happening, he wanted to help me.

'Are you all right?' he asked. 'Do you want to sit down for a while?'

All I can remember thinking was how much I hated him, hated him for what he did, hated him for what he was thinking, and I remember screaming and screeching at him, 'I hate you, I hate all men!' Now people were looking at us. We were, we had thought, at the rear of the coaches, out of sight of other passengers arriving, but many more had arrived and were now spreading out around us. I could see that several had probably witnessed what had happened and I could hear them tutting, but I was still in shock from what had happened, and suffering much discomfort in my stomach.

Somehow, we found ourselves back on the coach for the return journey home and not a word did we say to each other. I left the coach first and I never looked back. I remember it was late when I walked through the front door but not wanting my parents to suspect anything I shouted goodnight from the hallway, and went to bed.

I lay in bed, sobbing holding my stomach and talking in my mind to my unborn child, saying I was sorry, asking God to forgive me, praying that the baby would be all right, asking why everyone hated me. Was God punishing me for getting pregnant again? I felt so self-pitying and so sad that there wasn't anyone there to hold my hand and say, 'Don't worry, everything will be all right,' and eventually I fell asleep.

The days came and went but nothing happened while I waited every minute of every day for a miscarriage, for some sign to say that something was wrong, but there was nothing, apart from my feeling a little sore around my stomach. In a way it made me feel worse, for I would now worry for the rest of the pregnancy, wondering all the time if the baby would be born normal. A week had gone by since the coach trip and I had mellowed toward Denis as I always did. I had been so used to hidings in my life that I had learned to accept them as normal. I went to see him at his lodgings and I remember approaching him and saying how sorry I was. Can you believe that? I was sorry! And I asked him to take me back, in fact I can remember begging him to take me back, promising him all the things under the sun if only he would. I don't know why I did this. All I know is I did. I remember thinking only that I didn't want to be alone, I couldn't cope alone, I hated being alone—it was like being in the dark; it made me feel very frightened.

I remember we sat that night, all cosy, planning what we were going to do and he had said in a flippant sort of way, 'Well we have to get married.' Although he had calmed down a little about the whole situation, he made it quite clear that I would have to make all the arrangements. He didn't have time, with his long work hours. There was also the matter of me telling my parents. Although I knew that I was much older now, and more or less in charge of my own life, because of my previous history I knew in my heart that my stepfather would use anything he could to humiliate me.

I remember Denis and I discussing the whole matter over and over again, until late that evening, and I felt like I was playing mothers and fathers and thought at the time that I was very grown-up and mature. Yet I was very much the opposite, quite immature. I remember going home that evening feeling much more relieved holding my stomach and whispering to my unborn child, 'Don't worry, everything will be all right.'

Now that I had some definite plans, and Denis' assurance that he would marry me, I felt more able to approach my parents. First, I told my mother and to my surprise she responded quite well. I remember her saying, 'Well at least you will be getting married this time; your father will be pleased about that,' and she went on to say that there was no way that they could afford to pay for a wedding, and as long as it was understood that we paid for everything ourselves then that was fine with her. I felt that there was no warmth in her voice, only relief, relief that I would be another worry out of the way. Of course I still had my stepfather to tell but I knew that my mother would probably mention it to him and that would soften the blow for me. I told him that evening when he came home from work, waiting until he had his tea, as I had got to know over the years that this was the best time to talk to him about anything. I remember he sat with his feet up in his armchair by the fire because although it was late April, there was still a nip in the air. I walked up to him and just like a young child would approach her school teacher and ask to be excused I said, 'Dad, can I talk to you, please?' I was thinking how important manners were when talking to him and if any of us ever spoke without a please or thank you to him, he would punish us.

'What is it now?' he replied. 'If it's money, no, you have your own the same as I do.'

'No, it's not money, Dad,' I said. 'I'm getting married,' and with that he sat upright, looked directly at me and said, 'Getting married? What's brought this on?'

I remember standing there shaking and saying, 'I'm having a baby, Dad.' He looked away and picking up his newspaper he mumbled, 'Then you had better get married then, but don't expect me to pay for it.' He started to read the paper; nothing more was said, that being his signal that I was now dismissed and that he had nothing more to say. I walked away into the kitchen and breathed a sigh of relief because I didn't care that he wouldn't pay. I was just so pleased that I had told them both now, and that there had been no shouting or yelling and calling me names. I remember feeling quite excited inside and thinking to myself, 'I am going to be married, and have a baby, and a place of my own.'

It never crossed my mind that I was going to marry someone who had been violent to me and that maybe I would be going from the frying pan into the fire as I had done so many times before. Perhaps because it was the only way of life that I knew. I didn't want to see anything bad, I just blanked it all out of my mind, ignored it. I loved him, I kept telling myself. Yes, there had been bad times, but, now everything was going to be different; we were going to get married and have a baby. I convinced myself this would make everything wonderful. In my heart I would always make excuses for him but in my mind I was always fearful of him.

Once again my life was about to take a new direction and I felt frightened, but often found myself too busy to think about it. All the arrangements for the wedding had to be made. We had chosen a date the following month so that gave me very little time to fit in all that had to be done. I decided to hire a white wedding dress and bridesmaid's dresses for my two sisters who had agreed to be bridesmaids. My younger brother had been chosen by Denis to be his best man. A friend at work had offered to do the flowers at a low price for me and I bought several boxes of cards, also at a reduced price, and I set about making a list of guests. Denis had not been forthcoming with money for expenses but if I asked for amounts of money he would ask me what it was for, then nearly always hand it over. We had discussed together the wedding list and realised there would be over one hundred people on the invitation list, but had decided to keep it that way, as we hoped it would mean more wedding presents for us. Of course Roy and his wife and family would be among the guests, as would Sean and Flo and their new arrival, their baby daughter. Denis' mother had been excited with our news and had promised to fly over for the wedding. She had written in her last letter to me how she knew that her son Denis loved me very much and as long as I would be understanding towards him, everything would be fine. She went on to say that, even though she adored him, his father had died whilst she was very young and had asked Denis at the tender age of only five to take care of his mother and young brother. She explained how that had been quite a strain on a five-year-old child.

I still had fond memories of her and I was very pleased that she was able to come to our wedding and as with most weddings, it would be a good opportunity for her to meet my family.

It was to be a church wedding. As Denis and his family were all Catholics, and at that time the ruling of the Catholic church was anyone who married a Catholic would become a convert and promise to bring up all children that were born from the marriage into the Catholic faith. I promised to do this as I was, and had always been, a believer in God, so it made very little difference to me what faith I believed in. I had gone to Methodist Sunday school as a young child. I had been confirmed Church of England in the children's home in Australia; now I was to become a Roman Catholic. It more or less seemed like different days of the week to me.

All the arrangements had been made and the wedding day was getting very close: a few days to go, and it would be Saturday, my wedding day. It was hard to believe, and one of my friends at work had said as a joke one day, 'What if he doesn't turn up?'

I couldn't believe that she had said it and I remember horrible thoughts going through my mind and the only thing I could do was, as I always did, blank them out.

Being three months gone, I was starting to show, and that of course gave the neighbours something to talk about. I remember overhearing a few remarks like, 'This isn't the first time, you know.' 'I wonder how long this will last,' said another, but nothing could spoil my dreams; this was my wedding day, and I was going to have a husband and live in a small furnished flat that we had managed to rent within five miles of my parents' house. I couldn't help thinking at the time how strange it was that with all that I had been through with my parents I still wanted to be near them.

The big day arrived and I remember all the hustle and bustle going on downstairs. My mother had got up early and was organising the food to take to the hall as we had all joined in and prepared it the night before. Denis had gone back to his lodgings that night and I remember my mother saying that it was bad luck to see the bride before the wedding.

Most of our time that morning of the wedding was taken up with my two sisters, the bridesmaids. They were very much alike in their looks so we had arranged for a hairdresser to come in and put their long hair up and trim it with small white flowers. They both wore long turquoise satin dresses and, having dark complexions and black hair, I remember they looked beautiful, I was so proud of them. Then it was my turn to get ready and I remember I had a long white, short-sleeved, full-skirted dress, V-shaped at the waist to allow for my, now quite bulging, tummy. My head-dress was a circle of white flowers, with a white lace veil and my bouquet was of red roses and lily of the valley. I remember standing in front of the mirror and looking at myself and feeling like a millionaire. The family had gathered around me and there were lots of oohs and aahs. Someone said, 'Don't forget to breathe in when you're standing in front of the priest,' and like most girls, I would imagine, on their wedding day, I was getting a lot of attention. I remember we were all about to leave for the church and one of my sisters suddenly pulled her hair down, ruffled it all up and walked back into the house, saying she didn't want to be a bridesmaid, and there was a bit of a commotion. My mother said it was probably because she was nervous and that it was nothing for me to fret over. They fixed her hair and she was ready to leave for the church.

The whole day was lovely, everything went well and looking at the family together, everyone in their best attire, all talking and making speeches, laughing and joking, and small children running around in their little smart outfits, Sean and Flo with their new baby daughter, Ma from Dublin, so proud of her son getting married, but feeling a bit sad that the wedding was not in Ireland, Roy and his wife and their two small children, all my friends and my parents' friends, and Denis and I now husband and wife and I remember thinking, who in this world would look down on us today and believe all the turmoil that had gone on in my life. It seemed to me that everyone changes into somebody else just for wedding days but why couldn't life be like this every day? Even my stepfather was going around smiling and mixing and generally looking as if he was enjoying himself...maybe he was...who knows? But whatever it was, I was enjoying it for it seemed that for all the days of my twenty-three years, someone had saved up all the attention that I had missed out on and given it all to me in one day.

At the end of a glorious day, Denis and I went back to our newly rented furnished flat. There was no honeymoon, as we both had to be back at work on the following Monday but I didn't mind; I had had my wonderful day and would now look forward to having my baby.

I loved being a wife as I fussed over him, always trying to surprise him, sometimes with only a pack of cigarettes, or something special for tea. I polished and shone the flat, put up pretty curtains, giving the flat a cosy and warm feeling. He had always been a hard worker and worked very long hours and I remember we never got to see very much of each other although I would be home from work early tea-time and get everything prepared for him. Sometimes he wouldn't arrive home until after ten in the evening so his tea would be all dried up from trying to keep it warm over a saucepan of boiling water. If he was in a good mood when he came in he would eat it but if he was in a not-so-good mood he would shout at me, 'What do you call this? I work bloody hard all day and come home to this,' and with that he would pick up the plate and throw it at the wall, or across the room, before walking out the door and, I assume, going to the local pub. I remember this happening several times and I was always glad that he did walk out. That way I felt safe, if only for a while, for I knew that, after a few hours, he would be back through the door, having had a few drinks—shouting and yelling, knocking over anything that was in his way. Eventually, if I was lucky, he would go to bed and fall asleep. Denis was definitely a Jekyll and Hyde; sometimes really trying to be a good husband, and at other times just unbearable.

I learned to take the good with the bad; having done this for so many years with my life it came naturally. I only had one thing on my mind and that was the birth of my baby. I had worried secretly all through my pregnancy as to whether the baby would be all right, especially after the hard blow I had received in the first couple of months, but I had been attending the local clinic regularly, and they had assured me that all was well. Towards the last few months of my pregnancy, I noticed that Denis had been going out most nights. He would come home from work, say he wasn't hungry, and get changed, and as I remember now, he would always start an argument, turn the whole thing around so that it was my fault, then storm out of the door. Somehow or other, I would stand there when he was gone, feeling guilty, guilty that I had driven him out.

Almost to the exact day the baby was due, I went into labour, so Denis took me to the local maternity home which I had been booked into earlier by the health clinic. After twenty-six hours of what I remember to be sheer agony, I gave birth to a beautiful baby girl, weighing seven pounds and seven ounces. There was a little bit of a panic at first because apparently the cord was wrapped around her neck three times and she was very blue, but after a few minutes the skills of the midwife soon put everything right and all was well. She was absolutely beautiful, everything you can imagine of a tiny, perfect baby and we named her Denise, after her father. Only moments after she was born, Denis came in to visit. He was so happy that it was all over, and looked pleased, although it was hard to tell as he was never one to show his affections.

Ten days in hospital, and mother and baby were checked out. It had been arranged for a nurse to visit me at home for the next ten days to show me how to manage with my new baby, and to keep a close eye on the baby, making sure there was a weight gain, and not a weight loss.

CHAPTER
NINE

Time moved on. Looking after a baby and a husband was hard work, but very rewarding and I adored her. Denis threw himself into work and going out with his friends, and although I was always there for him, I lived for my baby. My parents had visited me at home on one occasion, to see the baby, and I remember being really happy about their visit, as I had very few friends since I had left work. Although I had my baby, sometimes I craved for adult company. I wanted to explain to my parents that I was lonely, that my husband was never home, but I couldn't. I could always remember my mother saying to me just before I was to be married, 'Think yourself lucky, my girl, that he's marrying you, and that you'll have a roof over your head. You have no cause to complain.' I was thankful for their visit but said nothing. I started to write more often to Sean and Flo who were expecting their second child very shortly so we had much in common to write about. I was always promising them in my letters that we would visit them soon, but every time I mentioned it to Denis he would say he was far too busy with his work.

His mother came and stayed with us for a couple of weeks in the summer. Denise was eight months old now, and starting to sit up and really take notice. I remember Ma bringing lots of presents over from Ireland, clothes for the baby, and foodstuffs for us, and clothes for me. Before going back, she was to visit Sean and his wife in London, then fly back to Dublin from there.

I was always glad of her visits as we got on so well and she was so helpful with the baby, and always very generous. I remember shortly afterwards that Denise had her first birthday. My two sisters who were now nineteen and twenty helped me to arrange a party. Most of the family were there and I remember Roy coming over for the day with his wife and family. I never saw him very often after I was married. There just wasn't any money then to use on travelling and it seemed that, once you were married and had a family, you stayed at home to look after them. I remember being happy to see him, remarking on how much his younger son looked like him when he was a small boy.

It was about two months after Denise's first birthday party that she started to get sick and I took her to the doctor. He gave her some medicine and said the usual—if she didn't improve I should bring her back. She didn't improve, so I took her back, and over the next four or five weeks I took her to the doctor almost weekly; on one occasion he accused me of becoming paranoid over my baby's health. Then, but only after I had insisted, the doctor sent her to hospital for some tests and they found that she had a nasty ear infection, gave me some drops and tablets and sent me home. Seventeen months old now, Denise was still being sick on a daily basis and I remember the doctor visiting and then ringing for an ambulance to take her to hospital because he suspected she had gastro-enteritis and would have to go into an isolation ward. I went in the ambulance with Denise to the hospital because I was so afraid something bad would happen to her. I had flashbacks of when that strange lady came and took Heidi from me and I remember holding Denise so tight and saying to myself, 'Please God, don't take her from me.' I remember promising God that I would do anything, anything in the whole wide world, if only he wouldn't take my baby from me.

Before long she was settled into a nice warm cosy hospital bed, and after the doctors had finished examining her, I rocked her gently, and she fell asleep. I had been sitting with her for quite some time, when a nurse came in and said it would be a good time for me to go home and she promised me she would take care of her; everything would be all right. I remember thinking those same words had already come back once to haunt me so I checked with the visiting times and said I would probably be back that evening with my husband, and I, very reluctantly, left. I hadn't been able to contact my husband that day because I wasn't sure what site he was working at and I knew that he wouldn't be able to do anything until he had finished work for that day. When he came home that evening, fortunately early, I told him what was wrong and asked if we could both go to the hospital that evening to visit our baby. I remember his response:. 'She is in the best hands,' he said. 'There is no point in travelling all that way, she will probably be asleep.'

I started to cry and he did try to comfort me but all I wanted was to be with my baby and to my own surprise I looked at him and said, 'Well, if you won't go, then I will go on my own.' Only after I had said this did I realise the hospital was a long way away, at least two bus rides; it was a country hospital especially designed for cases needing isolation. His only reply was, 'By the time you get there it will be time to come back,' and his selfishness and unconcern made me more determined. I got up from the chair, and quickly got myself ready, and shouted out as I was going to the door, for fear of him stopping me, 'I'm going now, bye.' I had no idea how I was going to get there, but the love of your own child along with determination can work wonders, and it did. I arrived on the second bus right outside the main entrance, feeling very pleased with myself, and eager to see my baby daughter.

I almost started to run through the hospital grounds, when I heard this voice shout out to me, 'Hi, wait for me.' I looked around and it was my husband pulling up in his car by the main gate and I couldn't believe my eyes. I remember calling him all the names under the sun, under my breath. He had made me come all this way on two buses, worried out of my mind, and he tootles up in the car like nothing has happened. How could he do this, I thought? But as I walked slowly towards him, I knew that I wouldn't be brave enough to say what I was thinking.

'Hang on,' he said. 'I'll park the car and we can go in together.' I wanted to say how much I hated him but I was only concerned with how my baby was; maybe later he would tell me why he did this to us, his wife and his daughter.

Denise was poorly, but comfortable, although very grizzly so I nursed her for as long as I could and I was pleased that her dad nursed her, and all my hatred of him once more disappeared. When it was time to leave, we had to get a nurse to stay with her in case she got upset and leant over and fell out of the cot bed.

Neither of us said very much to one another on the journey home but I remember in my thoughts that I began to make excuses for him. He worked hard, and I knew he hated hospitals so I began to tell myself that I was making a fuss over nothing, people all over the world were coping with ups and downs in their lives; why couldn't I? There was always someone out there a lot worse off than me so I wiped the tears from my eyes and told myself to be thankful for what I had.

Denise had been in hospital for a week now, and I visited as much as I could during the daytime, and then, if time permitted him, Denis would take me in the evenings.

I remember on this particular day, I had sat with her for most of the day. The nurse had given me the news that she was now getting better, although it had been very much touch and go at first as she had been very dehydrated. They had cleared the germ from her system and she was now on the road to recovery. I was really eager to give Denis the news that evening when I got home and he was happy to hear it. I remember I made something special for tea to celebrate that Denise would probably be home in a few more days.

We had just sat down, cuddled up to one another, when the doorbell rang, so I got up to answer it. 'Telegram,' the young man said. 'Sign here, please.' I remember taking the pen, signing my name, closing the front door and standing frozen to the spot in the hallway.

I was startled by my husband's voice: 'Who is it?' he shouted. I walked slowly towards him. 'It's a telegram,' I said.

He jumped up from the sofa. 'Telegram,' he yelled. 'From who?'

By this time I was standing beside him holding this telegram outstretched in my hand. We both stood still staring at each other knowing that telegrams nearly always carried bad news.

'Open it,' he said.

'No, you open it,' I replied and he took the telegram from me.

'Give me the damn thing,' he said, and he tore it open, and read out loud: 'Sean, accident, serious, ring hospital, Flo.'

It was dreadful. We stared at each other for I don't know how long. We had no phone so he said he would drive to the nearest phone box, yelling at me to hurry up. We got into the car; his driving always scared me at the best of times, but this time I felt like I was taking off in a jumbo jet as he drove like a maniac to the phone box. He leapt from the car, almost before he had stopped, and ran for the phone box. I remember there was an elderly lady in the box talking on the phone so he grabbed her, hauling her from the phone. She almost fell on top of me but I explained to her what had happened, and I remember she was very kind and understanding, and said she would go and find another phone. Whilst I had been outside calming the elderly lady, he had phoned a London hospital. For the rest of my life I shall always remember the look on his face when he came out of that phone box and he said to me, 'Sean is unconscious, something fell from a hoist at work and hit him on the head and he is not expected to live.'

These words 'not expected to live' went over and over in my mind and I could see how angry Denis was. I was so afraid to speak; I was afraid to move; I began to cry.

'Get in the car,' he said, and somehow we arrived home, I don't remember how. We went into the house and he said we had to go straight to London.

I remember my head was spinning, and I was trying to put things into perspective. I loved Sean like he was my own brother and I remember trying to visualise him in my mind, to picture the last time I saw him. It was awful. I couldn't; I couldn't concentrate. I suddenly thought of Denise being in hospital and I must have blurted out, 'I can't go now, who will look after Denise?'

'Then I will go,' he said. I pleaded with him to calm down and to sit down together and sort out the best thing to do. He immediately went into a rage, tipping over furniture in the living room and he punched the walls until his knuckles were bleeding. He smashed everything in sight but I knew how he was feeling. I also felt like that, but this outburst and all this damage wasn't going to help Sean. I quickly suggested that I would ring my youngest brother, Rodney, who had become very friendly with Denis since he had been best man at our wedding, and Denis seemed to respond a little to my suggestion.

'Sit there,' I said, 'I will go and use the neighbours' phone.' Every part of my body was shaking as I went next door and rang their bell.

They had always been very good neighbours and as she opened the door I asked if could use her phone. 'Certainly,' and I think the look of desperation on my face was self-explanatory.

I rang my brother at work and after what seemed to be forever he came to the phone and after I explained what had happened, he said he would leave work there and then and would drive straight over to our house. I thanked my neighbour and hurriedly went back to my husband. I walked back into my own living room and remember thinking how it looked as though a bomb had gone off. I found Denis still sitting in the armchair staring into space, saying over and over to himself, 'Oh please God let him be all right.'

I didn't have time to express my emotions; it was all I could do to keep my husband calm, and I remember thinking to myself, 'Why can't I be the one to go to pieces, to let myself go? Why do I always have to be the one to hold myself together for someone else?' Then I remember pulling myself together, and feeling guilty for having selfish thoughts. I explained to Denis that my brother was on the way, and that perhaps they could then make plans to travel to London. That way he would be safer with someone else driving and have someone to talk to.

Within the next hour Rodney turned up and they left for London. They said they would ring and leave a message with our neighbours, as I explained that I would be at the hospital until late with Denise.

After they had left, I remember I took time to sit down with a cup of tea and try to take in all that had happened in the last few hours. I prayed so hard that Sean would be all right—only twenty-four years of age, married with two young daughters. I tried to think of what Flo was going through, and who was minding her two baby girls, and then I suddenly thought about Sean and Denis' mother in Ireland. Denis had said something to me after he had made the phone call about Flo having notified their mother and that she was getting the first available plane over. I remember thinking how one's life can be so simple one minute and then in a complete turmoil the next.

I looked up at the clock and saw that it was time for me to leave to catch the first bus to the hospital to visit Denise. I really can't remember how I got to the hospital that day. Looking back now, communication in those days was very difficult, there being only a few houses with telephones. Mobile phones were, of course, unheard of so we just waited longer to get our news. I remember sitting in the hospital ward that night cuddling my child to me, rocking to and fro, asking God would he please take care of Sean and his family.

After the visit, the nurse gave me the good news that Denise could go home in a few days providing she continued to make good progress. I remember being thrilled, knowing I could cope so much better at home, especially now she was so much better.

I arrived home that evening feeling totally exhausted and tried to have a sleep before my husband and brother got back. I was very worried as I knew London was a long way to go and come back from in one short day. I managed to fall asleep around eleven and was woken with a start at three in the morning by the two of them coming through the front door. I jumped up, all blurry-eyed, and asked how Sean was and my brother put his arm around me and asked would I make a cup of coffee as the news was not good. My husband looked as though he was in a trance; he just sat in the chair and buried his head in his hands. I went over to him, put my arm around him and tried to comfort him as best I could.

By this time my brother was making the coffee and my husband began to explain what had happened to Sean. He had been working a late night shift to make some extra money and something went wrong with the hoist two storeys up, and it fell directly on Sean's head and they said that by the time it had hit him it would have weighed approximately six tons. With tears rolling down his face he went on to say that all one side of Sean's face was gone and that if he did survive—and apparently there was little chance that he would—he would most definitely have brain damage. I remember bursting into tears, and thinking how could I give him my good news that Denise would be home in a few days, so I decided it could wait until morning. I made up a bed on the sofa for my brother and thanked him for being with us. He looked exhausted from driving but he didn't seem bothered by all the smashed-up furniture; it was as if he expected it to be there. Neither of us got much sleep that night but a new day always seems to shed a different light on things. We all got up quite early considering the time we went to bed, and Denis made his way to the phone box to phone the hospital to see if there was any change in his brother's condition. He came back to say that there was no change and that he was on a life-support machine. He also said that his mother had arrived and that from the time she arrived she had not left her son's bedside.

Everything was very strained for the next few days, but there were some happy times for me. I brought Denise home from the hospital, and she looked so well. I was so overjoyed at having her home. I told myself, all I wanted now was for Sean to be well, and I would never ever complain of anything ever again. Sadly life doesn't always work out like that.

One week after his accident the doctors, with the permission of Flo and Ma, turned off the life support machine that was keeping Sean alive. I remember that day so well. All I wanted to do was scream and scream. I felt riddled with guilt that I hadn't gone to see him before he died, and I remember asking God, why, at that time, had he made me choose between my daughter and Sean? Then I quickly realised how selfish I was being, and my thoughts went to Flo and her two children, how she must be feeling. I remembered how happy they were together and how they planned to live and work in England, and 'oh God' what if they hadn't? Sean would be alive today. And what of his poor mother, who idolised him? I saw him in my mind hugging her, and laughing and joking. 'Don't worry, Ma, I'll be all right, you take care of yourself', he would always say. And now he was gone. That night Denis and I cried until we could cry no more.

We were soon to find out that as soon as they turned off the life support machine they asked Flo if they could they use Sean's heart for Britain's second heart transplant. She said no, that she couldn't bear the thought of Sean's heart beating inside someone else. However, both Sean and she had discussed donating organs during their marriage and she agreed to donate both his kidneys. They were used to save two people's lives.

The whole of that next week is a blur in my memory banks. How we managed to cope until the funeral I don't know. Looking back now, I was so grateful to have had Denise home from hospital, as she took our minds off some of the hardships.

Then Denise got sick again and I took her to the doctor who said he couldn't find anything wrong with her though he said she had a slight temperature, but not to worry. I was very concerned; she had already lost so much weight from being ill previously. I was trying to build her back up again, and what with everything else that had gone on I sometimes felt that I was going to go to pieces. Looking after my husband was like looking after another baby. He had been like a zombie since Sean's death and, with Denise being ill again, it wasn't as if he didn't care—he just couldn't cope.

The arrangements for the funeral were made. I was devastated since, because Denise was so unwell, I couldn't go. I had been in touch with Flo, explaining, and she was very understanding, and once again I felt riddled with guilt. I remember looking up at the sky and asking Sean to forgive me.

After the funeral Ma came to stay with us for a week before she went back to Dublin. I couldn't help thinking how terrible it was going to be for her going home alone, having to come to terms with the death of her youngest son.

As life slowly got back to as normal as possible, I had promised Flo that I would write to her often, and that we would always be there for her if she needed us.

Sean had died as a result of an accident at work, so now there would be an investigation, and, we hoped, Flo and her two children would be entitled to some compensation. But such things took time, and in the meantime she would have to manage as best she could. At the same time, friction arose between Flo and Ma, as to who should be entitled to any compensation. His mother thought it should be hers as Sean was her son, and Flo, of course, because she was his wife. There had always been niggly feelings between them as Ma had never forgiven her, as she put it, for taking Sean to England. So the bad feelings began to fester as rumour was that there was going to be a large sum of compensation.

I remember it all got very nasty between them, and Flo had received several threats from her late husband's mother so Flo decided to write to Ma and to Denis and me. In her letter she said that she didn't want to have anything to do with Ma ever again. My husband got very annoyed at this letter as obviously it was his mother too and he decided that neither of us would have contact with Flo and her two daughters ever again. To this day, thirty years on, I have never seen or heard from Flo and her two girls again. Isn't that just too sad even to contemplate?

Once again, life took on some sort of normality before disaster struck yet again. It was approximately five-thirty one evening when I was getting Denise ready for bed, and suddenly she went into what looked like a fit. I screamed out to Denis who was upstairs at the time, and he came running down and immediately went into a panic. He always reacted like this; he just could not seem to face up to any traumatic situation and he screamed at me, 'What's wrong with her? Do something,' he said.

'I don't know,' I replied. 'Go next door and ring the doctor,' I said.

'I can't,' he said, and taking Denise from me he said, 'You ring. I'll hold her and don't be long.'

I remember using the neighbours' phone and memories of Sean came rushing back to me. 'Oh please God, don't let her die,' I said to myself. Surgery hours were over and a nurse answered and asked me to keep calm, then said she would get the doctor to call. In the meantime she would tell me what to do to help my daughter. She said to go home and undress her, and splash tepid water over her, that she was convulsing because of a high temperature and cooling her down would bring down her temperature. I ran back home to confront my husband at the front door, finding him in a complete panic. He handed Denise to me, and again he said, 'Hurry, do something.' Trying to calm him and carry out the nurse's instructions, I didn't seem to have time to panic myself and once again I had to keep myself together to take control of the situation. After a few minutes Denise stopped convulsing and I remember cuddling her close to me, but not too close for fear of her starting again. I remember the doctor taking four hours to arrive. It was nearly ten o'clock that evening and he apologised for his delay and examined Denise. He said that he couldn't find anything wrong with her that would cause her to have the high temperature, which in turn was the cause of the convulsions. Then he went on to say that he had found a few spots behind her ears, which, he said, could be the start of measles but he wasn't sure. He told me to give her something to keep her temperature down and to keep her cool. I remember his exact words were, 'Just keep a sheet over her, get a good night's sleep and she will be right as rain in the morning,' and he left.

I remember not putting Denise in her bed upstairs. Instead, I made a bed up on the settee for her; that way we would both hear her if she woke or something went wrong. I laid out a nice cool cotton sheet, and then lay Denise just in her nappy on top, then another cool cotton sheet over her. It was the month of July so the air temperature was warm. She soon fell asleep, and we had our tea and watched television. Later that evening, when it was time for us to go to bed, we decided to bring our mattress downstairs on the floor beside the settee so as not to disturb Denise. Because we were still so worried about what had happened to her earlier that evening, we wanted to be near her all the time. I remember lying beside her, holding her hand, and, eventually, we fell asleep.

It was pitch dark when I awoke with a start and I looked at the clock. It was three o'clock in the morning and I reached out to hold Denise's hand and I knew, I knew straightaway that something was wrong so I jumped up, yelling and waking my husband. I remember screaming, 'She's dead. My baby is dead.' I tried resuscitating her but I didn't really know how—only from what I had read or seen on television. It was a nightmare; my husband was ranting and raving behind me, banging his head on the wall, and I could hear him saying over and over again, 'Please God, no.' It was a living hell as we were running out into the street yelling for help. One neighbour came out and called for an ambulance, another came over to comfort me, and after what seemed like a lifetime, the ambulance arrived and they carried Denise into the ambulance. One of the ambulance men helped me into the ambulance and then turned to my husband and asked him to drive his car to the hospital, which, fortunately, was only a few miles from us.

I don't remember anything that happened in the ambulance, only arriving at the hospital and being told to wait and that the doctor would be with me as soon as he could. I knew that my baby was dead, but I hoped, I hoped and prayed with all my heart that I was wrong. When I saw the doctor walking towards me, I knew. He told me how sorry he was, that there was nothing

110

that they could do and that she had been dead on arrival. He went on to say that he would take me to see her but I don't know how I got there. I only remember standing in a small room with a hospital bed and lying in that bed just like she was sleeping, was my beautiful baby daughter. I sobbed and I sobbed until there were no more tears and I leaned over and kissed her. I remember she was so cold—just like a china doll, I thought. I looked up and I asked God why. Why did he take my baby? She was only one year and six months old so why was he punishing me? I remember thinking he had taken two of my babies now, why? At that moment I felt an arm on my shoulder; it was my husband. I remember him saying how strange it was that nobody had told him where Denise and I were, but he had parked his car outside the hospital and just walked straight to us. We both looked at each other and we knew, we just knew, that it was Sean who had guided him to us.

Our baby was dead but I couldn't believe it; it was like the end of the world for me. My husband threw himself into his work and I couldn't begin to think how he felt losing a brother and a daughter in one month. I could only think of myself and how I felt and as every day passed I just sat and cried, holding her toys or folding her clothes and I kept asking God, why? Why was all this happening? How could he bless you with such a lovely child and then just take that child away? It didn't seem right, but with all these questions going around in my head I didn't blame God. I kept my faith; I just wanted to know why. I thought that he could have taken me or my husband, but he took an innocent child, not yet two years old. Why?

My parents and family were exceptional at arranging the funeral and although I don't remember much about it, I remember that they were all there for me, especially my brothers and sisters. I remember one of my sisters had had her first baby three weeks before Denise had died and my sister allowed me to cuddle her and look after her from time to time. I didn't feel any bitterness towards her because she still had her baby and I didn't,

111

because her baby was my niece and I loved her dearly and looking after her really helped me get on with my life.

My marriage was never very strong, and on reflection I believed it was very one-sided. I wanted someone to love me and I always made the mistake of thinking if I loved someone that someone would love me in return.

CHAPTER
TEN

Nothing seemed quite the same between us any more and I felt like I had fallen down a big hole, falling, falling, and never reaching the bottom. Days and months passed and my other sister was expecting her first baby and I was reaching the stage where I really could have snatched someone else's baby. I knew I wanted another baby more than anything in the whole world and I remember saying my prayers each night and promising God that I would be good if he would give me another chance.

After only seven months of waiting I got my chance. I was pregnant and I couldn't believe it. I remember feeling so lucky and I told everyone in the family of my good news, and, of course, my husband who was also pleased, pleased especially that he would no longer have to come home from work and see me crying. I was so happy I didn't know what I had ever done wrong but I knew now that, whatever it was, I had been forgiven; I was pregnant. My memories of my pregnancy are wonderful because I felt so well and even friends and family remarked on how well I looked. Most people I knew talked about how nice it would be if I had a little boy so, they would say, that I wouldn't be able to make comparisons with Denise. That made me feel good as I remember often touching my tummy and talking to my unborn child as if it was Denise and I was going to get her back. I explained, several times, to my husband how I felt and he would just say I was mad, going crazy, he said. It was then that my whole outlook changed and I did start looking forward to having a little baby by concentrating on boys' names and clothes for a boy. I began to feel better and my headaches that I had had for some time were disappearing and I felt healthy. My husband continued to work hard day and night so we hardly ever saw much of each other. This was his way of dealing with his pain and when he got home from work he would nearly always go out down the local pub with his friends or play in a darts match.

Life had gone on. We had moved into a house just before Denise had died and now we had a nice garden and I would spend most of my time working in the garden and although I was pregnant I remained active, always taking care not to harm my unborn child.

The big day arrived. I was to have the baby at home, which was quite usual in those days for pregnant mothers without any complications. I had started my pains at around six-thirty this middle of August day and the midwife came to examine me and I always remember her saying, 'Oh! You have ages to go yet, my dear. I've got time to put my curlers in and take my tights off.' We laughed together, then she proceeded to do exactly what she had said. My youngest sister, who had promised to come over and stay with me for a couple of days, just in case, was downstairs. I remember the midwife telling my husband and my sister's husband to go to the pub and come back around ten-thirty while my sister busied herself with her own baby downstairs.

At five past eleven I gave birth to a beautiful baby boy weighing in at seven pounds and like most mothers my first question was, 'Is he all right?'

'He's perfect,' the midwife replied. As I held him and looked lovingly into his tiny self I remember feeling so full of love for him. He was to be my new beginning.

I wanted to stand on the roof and yell at the top of my voice to the world that I had a new baby son and, although this was probably happening to thousands of mothers every single minute of each day, I still felt like I was the only one in the whole world who had just had a new baby. I had heard my husband come in only minutes before his son was born, and he came up the stairs and nervously entered the room whereupon the midwife said, 'You have a son and he is fine.'

She pointed to the crib where Paul, our new son, lay sleeping and I remember my husband looked at me and said, 'Well done,' and through his smile I saw some of the pain disappear from his face.

I can't find words enough to explain the happiness I felt during the next few weeks. There was no improvement in my unstable marriage but this, for the first time since the wedding, didn't seem to bother me any more. I had given my husband so much love over the years and I had only ever received rejection in return, there being so many times during my marriage that he had been violent and cruel to me. I had said to him on several of those occasions that I would stop loving him, that he would make me hate him, and although we both shared this beautiful son my feelings grew less and less for my husband and more and more for my son. Getting married for better and for worse in those days meant exactly that, so life went on for us as husband and wife.

When Paul was six weeks old I took him to the local health centre for his usual check-up, and after the nurse had weighed him, measured him and said that everything was fine, I took him in to see the doctor as the final part of his check-up. She examined him, then asked me to sit down and I felt my stomach rise into my throat. 'Oh my God,' I said, 'what's wrong with him?'

The doctor explained to me that Paul had a heart murmur and she wanted to send him for tests, but asked me not to worry. I remember thinking how many times I had heard that before and I picked up my baby, and cuddled him closely and I felt the tears start to roll down my cheek. The doctor fetched me a nurse who came very quickly and took me to another room to make a hospital appointment and did her best to comfort me at the same time. I remember pushing my baby home in the pram sobbing and talking out loud to myself and my new baby, Paul.

I always went home past the cemetery where Denise was buried, it being so near to our house and I remember I got to the grave, where a nice headstone was now installed with a beautiful photograph of Denise engraved into it. Then I spoke to Paul of his sister, how much I loved her, and how I would always remember her, and how I prayed that she would always be his guardian angel. Then, before I left, I prayed to God that he would send Denise our guardian angel to watch over Paul and keep him safe and free from all harm.

My new appointment was in one week, and the waiting during that one week seemed forever. Eventually the day arrived and I had to take Paul to the main children's hospital thinking, 'Why did they always build things for children up hills or upstairs?' The appointment was more or less on time and I remember being called in to see the specialist. After a thorough examination and x-rays and all the things that doctors do that we don't understand, I sat with Paul on my lap listening to what the doctor had to say.

'Your son has a hole in his heart,' he said and I felt my arms tighten around my baby so much that I might have hurt him. The doctor went on to explain that Paul's heart had a hole in one side and blood was leaking from this hole into his lungs. 'At the moment,' he said, 'he can cope with the amount of blood but we will keep a close eye on him and when he gets older we will operate. It will be a simple procedure,' he said, and his exact words were, 'It will be just like mending a bicycle puncture.' He asked me several questions. 'Did Paul turn blue at any time?' he asked. I'm not sure how I answered any of his questions. I just sat fixed in the chair until those famous words came. 'Don't worry, everything will be all right.'

I got up to leave and the doctor said, 'Make an appointment with the nurse at the reception on your way out.' I went home that day feeling very much alone but I did ring my sisters because we had a phone in the house now. Since Denise died I had been very close to them; they always seemed there for me and now they had children of their own they could understand how I was feeling. I didn't see much of my mother and stepfather. I suppose this was so because we had never been close during my childhood but it was too late to try and make amends now. My younger brother was also very much in my life at that time but I heard that Roy was having problems with his marriage and somehow, as these last few years had gone by, we had lost touch with each other. I think he was trying to find himself and someone to love him much the same as I was. My eldest brother Alan had emigrated to Canada shortly after he married and although I did write to him several times, I got no response.

Denis, my husband was by now totally involved with his work and saving money. I found he would always listen to what I had to say but hear nothing. I was still very much in touch with his mother but didn't want to give her anything to worry about, knowing that she was far away. There was nothing she could do and she would only sit and worry, having never been quite the same since her son and granddaughter had died. I couldn't bring myself to tell her about Paul, not yet anyway.

It turned out that Paul, despite his heart problem, was a healthy happy baby, there being no physical signs of his condition, so therefore it disappeared to the back of my mind and lay dormant for most of the time. Each time I took him for a check-up they would say, 'He's fine, we will just continue to watch his progress.' I would worry for a while, then everyday life would take over until the next appointment, which, after his first birthday was only twice a year as the doctor had said they were pleased with his progress.

I remember Paul nearly being two years of age when I was about to have another baby. I was thrilled, to be pregnant again. I loved children and although I had more problems with my marriage I was still pleased to be having another baby. I always remember an elderly lady saying to me one day that every time her husband hung his trousers over the bed at night she got pregnant and I think that's how it was with me, and maybe with most women in those days.

My next baby was born in the local hospital and weighed in

at six pounds ten ounces, I had been gardening when my waters broke, followed by the pains, and before I knew it a friend had taken me to hospital and I had another son. He was adorable; as fair as Paul was, our new son Sean was dark. Although my marriage was still very strained, we had both decided that the time was right and that we would call our new baby Sean, after his Uncle Sean who had died in the accident. Life again returned to normality and I was a very busy mother now with two lovely children and I loved every minute of it. This continued for another two years with many more ups and downs with my marriage, some serious, some just everyday things.

Then I was pregnant again, but to my husband it was now becoming a financial worry. As with Paul and Sean, I was thrilled. My sisters were very pleased for me and in turn were catching up with me in terms of children. We often went shopping and to coffee mornings together with our children and I have some very fond memories of the years we were all having our children. We spent a lot of time together and the children, who were cousins to each other, grew up very close to one another. On several occasions we visited my parents but my mother didn't seem to have the maternal bond with her grandchildren that I would have liked her to have. Looking back now, I think my mother had too many problems of her own. My stepfather was up to his old tricks again, favouring his two daughters' children. After all, he would say to me, they were his real grandchildren and mine were not. On many occasions it became very obvious that he was being horrible to my children, much the same as he was to me when I was a child, but somehow, and, don't ask me why, I fought on and on to gain some sort of recognition from him.

My third baby was due on Easter Monday and, to the exact day, I went into labour. I went by ambulance to the same local hospital and this time after a bit of a struggle I gave birth to a beautiful baby girl. I loved my sons with all my heart and now, to have a daughter, to have another chance at having a daughter, I couldn't believe it. I thanked God for his kindness and we

118

named her Wendy, and once more I remember thinking that the rain in my life had disappeared and the sun had come out again.

Wendy was idolised by her two little brothers and they watched over her tentatively. She walked at a very young age and I was the happiest mother in the whole world. I would walk to the shops with one in the pram and one either side, feeling so proud and feeling that after all these years I had at long last been forgiven. Forgiven for what, I didn't know, but I can remember thinking I must have done something wrong to have been punished so, and now everything was all right.

I was still visiting Denise's grave, approximately every six to eight weeks, and I would take the children with me and talk to them about how their sister was and how she was now an angel and how her and their Uncle Sean were their guardian angels and would always watch over them all and keep them safe. I remember whilst I was arranging the flowers they would fetch the water for me and right up to this very day I always find peace and contentment at the cemetery where Denise is buried. Looking after three small children was quite a task. Although I loved every minute of them, there were obviously times when it wasn't all easy. I was still taking Paul for his annual check-ups at the hospital and taking all three on the bus with a pushchair and walking up the steep hill to the hospital entrance was hard work. I remember that the buses all had conductors in those days. Some of them were so helpful that they would get off the bus, pick up the pushchair and put it in the luggage rack, whilst others would ring the bell for the driver to drive off before I had chance to get organised and I would look up and the bus would be gone.

These were everyday things that everyday people went through and life for me went on much the same as it did for others. My husband was going out every evening by now. He didn't want to be a married man with three children, he wanted to be a single man again. On one occasion, when we were on an outing with his local darts team, I remember him saying, 'Don't walk with me; I don't want everyone to see that I am straddled with a wife and three kids.' And I accepted it, having gone along with his way of thinking for so long, out of sheer fear of him. I would become a sort of actress when he was around, and when he wasn't there, I became myself again.

One of my worst memories is the telephone call I received in the middle of the night from my sister, to say that my mother had had a suspected stroke and was in hospital, unconscious. I remember how hard it was for me to make the arrangements just to go to the hospital to be with her because of the marriage problems I was having and, of course, three young children to look after. Eventually I managed to get a sitter from next door and my husband drove me to the hospital. Walking into the hospital was a sad reminder of when my daughter Denise had died and I remember feeling quite anxious. When we eventually got to the ward, all I remember is that the screens were around my mother and the family were sitting around the bed and the first person I spotted was Roy. He was holding Mum's hand and talking to her, trying to get her to respond. Apparently Mum had been to a bingo session, something she had become very fond of in the last few years, and she had won the jackpot prize of one hundred pounds. I am only assuming, like the rest of the family, that she rushed to get home to share her good news, and, upon arriving home, found her husband out. She had presumably felt unwell and gone to bed. Apparently, he came in later and found her unconscious, then panicked and drove to my sister to tell her and an ambulance was finally called.

I don't know why but I don't remember much about my mother dying. I know that she didn't regain consciousness and after three days she died. I know that everyone in the family was upset, especially Roy. I remember feeling confused, part of me feeling that my mother had been robbed of her life as she had only reached sixty-one years of age, the other part of me feeling that I had been robbed, robbed of my mother's love. I never really knew my mother and I never felt that she knew or loved me. There was so much I wanted to know from her. Why did she never sit down and talk to me of what had happened all those years ago and try and explain why she had sent us away? Why did she never say sorry to me for the way my stepfather treated me? I was her child, she was my mother and I would have thought that would be important to her. Now she was dead and she could never ever tell me that she loved me. For a while I remember feeling all the sadness of the past well up in my throat and I wanted to cry for my mother but I couldn't. I could only cry for the mother that I'd wanted.

I cannot describe my mother's funeral because I don't remember it, and that makes me feel so ashamed. But as hard as I try I cannot remember it but I do remember standing there and day-dreaming of long ago, seeing myself as a small girl on a swing, swinging higher and higher and singing:

Goodbye mummy darling I miss you
Just like the stars that miss the sky
Although we had to part
You're always in my heart
Goodbye mummy darling goodbye.

The saying goes, three times is lucky, but for me four times was lucky, as I found myself pregnant again, although in the early stages of the first three months I remember I was quite upset that I was. My husband and I were arguing more and more and it was all I could do to get him to take notice of the three children I already had, let alone another. He was not very generous with money, so buying clothes and accessories was very difficult for me, and I found myself trying to keep up with my sisters. They both had new prams and clothes and I always had second-hand. Even when Paul was born and, after suffering all the upset of losing Denise, I could only afford my sister's second-hand pram and although my husband was probably earning more than their two husbands put together, he never felt it should be spent on his wife and family, not even just his children. I recall one time when I asked for money for two pairs of shoes for the boys and he put up every argument under the sun as to why they shouldn't have new shoes, the arguments so intense that we went three days without speaking. Finally, I left a note on the table for him, pleading with him to talk to me, that I was going mad with the silence, and I would say how sorry I was and would he please forgive me? On this particular day he must have got up early, read my note, which was gone, and in its place was a cheque for four hundred pounds. I had no idea at the time what it was for, only that it was made out to me and I remember worrying all day, wondering if he wanted me to get him some cash from the bank. As it was, I left the cheque there, being too scared to touch it. He came home that evening and very casually picked up the cheque and said, 'Here you are, that's for you to have some money of your own.' I just stood there scared out of my wits and said, 'No, that's all right, I only want a few pounds for the boys' shoes, just five pounds will do.'

'Go on, take it,' he said, but I didn't. I felt that there was a trick somewhere, and all that money! I kept telling myself he would only ask me what I had done with it and that would make us end up having a terrible argument and then another bout of silence. I handed him back the cheque and smoothed it over by saying, 'You keep it and if I want any money I will ask you for it, all right?'

'Suit yourself,' he said, taking the cheque and everything went back the way it had been, so I had my chance and some would say I 'blew' it.

I remember ringing my younger sister and saying, 'Guess what? I'm pregnant again,' and I said to her that I didn't want any more children and that I could hardly cope with the expense now. Everyone in my family suspected that my marriage wasn't too good but nobody said anything, and I never told all that went on. I wanted everyone to think that I was happy and that I had the best husband in the whole world.

I had been speaking to several friends who had told me that if I took very hot baths for three nights in a row, and bought some type of medicine from the chemist, swallowed two big spoonfuls and rubbed some on my stomach, in a clockwise direction, then swallowed a small glassful of gin—that all of this would take my pregnancy away. Shamefully, I must admit, I did all this. I can only thank God it didn't work, and, looking back now I'm not surprised, but at the time I was terrified, and, as my pregnancy continued each month, I became more and more worried, riddled with guilt and I felt that God would punish me. I felt sure he would give me a baby that had something wrong with it, and I prayed with all my might for his forgiveness for my wicked thoughts.

I had started my labour pains two weeks early and the ambulance took me to the same local hospital and after a relatively short time I gave birth to a beautiful baby boy, and he was perfect. I remember feeling so relieved, over the moon and he weighed in at seven pounds and two ounces. We named him Denis but because his father's name was also Denis it soon became very confusing and my younger sister nicknamed him Denny, and from then on he was always called Denny.

After a couple of days I was back home with my family and I can't describe how they all fussed over 'little Denny' and I remember looking at all four of them and thinking how lucky I was, nobody could ever hurt me again. I had four wonderful children who I loved so much and just for a second my mind flashed back to my mother and wondering how on earth she ever said goodbye to her children by sending us away to Australia.

I hadn't seen Roy for some time now, but I had heard that he had separated from his wife and was now with another girl and that she was expecting Roy's child. I remember thinking how sad it was that we had been so close at one time, and how we had drifted apart, as if we had been destined to be parted from each other. I knew that he had always been unsettled since he came back from Australia all those years ago but I didn't know all the scars he carried from that time. I knew that my own scars had not healed; they only lay dormant in the back of my mind. Every time I looked at my children, I tortured myself with the past, and I would say over and over, 'Nobody will ever take my children away and nobody will ever hurt them.'

Then one day after months and months of mental and physical abuse from my husband, he came home late one particular night and started ranting and raging. I remember that night so well; the children were all in bed asleep, I offered to make him a cup of coffee and I was willing to do anything to try and take his mind off me. He had been drinking, and the alcohol, I knew, made him bad-tempered. I always became terrified of him when he was like this because although he wasn't drunk, something in the alcohol made him angry. I remember he continued to shout abuse.

Apart from being scared of him, I had always been the perfect wife. I looked after him, I adored his children, I was always there for him, but this was never enough. He never trusted me, always accused me of seeing other men, accused me of letting in other men and hiding them in the loft. He had nailed all the windows down in the house, had written all over the walls— messages, sometimes hate messages, but other times how much he loved me; although it may sound strange, I did really believe that he loved me in his way. But this was obsession and I knew he needed help. I suggested it to him on this particular night and he went berserk and started to throw things around, smashing things, then the phone rang. It was late, twelve thirtyish and I remember him swearing, 'Who the bloody hell is that at this time? I expect it's one of your boyfriends,' and he went towards the phone. I heard him talking to one of his work-mates, and his whole tone of voice had changed. Anyone would think he was the nicest man in the whole world, and they did. Then, without thinking, I ran for the back door and ran down the street as fast as my legs could carry me. It was like when I was a child and my stepfather would say to me that the devil would get me if I was naughty so I ran and ran, as if the devil was chasing me, past about twenty houses.

I knocked at a friend's house, not thinking how late it was, I was so afraid, so desperate. She came to the door and I asked to use her phone. 'Come in,' she said and asked me what was wrong and I explained to her what had happened and how afraid of him I was, being even more afraid now because I had run away, and he would punish me further as I had taken our problems outside the house. A neighbour knew now and he hated anyone knowing how violent he was; he could change so quickly just like he did when he answered the phone, and everyone would think he was wonderful. He was a real Jekyll and Hyde. I used my friend's phone and telephoned my elder sister and after asking me if I was all right, she said, 'What about the children?'

Oh my God, I thought, my children! I thought how I had always promised them and myself that I would never ever leave them, whatever happened. I tried to ease my conscience by telling my sister that the children were all in bed asleep and that he would never harm them. I knew this to be true and although there were many times when he would mentally torture them with his violent outbursts he would never harm them physically. My sister asked me to stay where I was and that she and her husband would be right over to collect me. Living nearby, they were both with me within the next ten minutes and I remember my brother-in-law saying he would take me to the police station, which is what he did, explaining to me on the way that the police might not get involved as it was a domestic situation. I kept saying over and over, 'I must get my children.' We arrived at the local police station and I remember they were marvellous saying they would follow us to the house, which they did, and on arrival, a few minutes later, they asked my sister and her husband to stay in their car and asked me to follow them. They explained that they were going to get the children out of the house but I needed to be with them. I will always remember that night. There were three policemen and one policewoman and I was frightened out of my wits as we walked towards the front door and they rang the bell.

My husband answered the door and in a very calm and concerned voice he said, 'Oh there you are, I've been so worried about you, where have you been?' The three policemen said that they wanted no trouble that they were there just to get the children and they held him to one side, not physically but just by talking to him and surrounding him. The policewoman and I went upstairs and woke the children and one by one took them to my sister and her husband in the car. I was absolutely terrified, more so now that I had gone this far, for he had always promised me that if I ever left him he would get me because if he couldn't have me nobody else ever would. As I walked down the stairs, I could hear him ranting and raving to the police, and above it all he shouted out, 'You had better look over your shoulder because wherever you are, I will be there,' and I knew that he meant me. My sister and her husband assured the police that we would be all right and that we could stay with them until things were sorted and shortly afterwards the children were tucked up in makeshift beds and myself with them. My sister and her husband said goodnight and that we would talk about arrangements in the morning.

CHAPTER
ELEVEN

Another very sad part of my life was to emerge from that night. After a separation time there was to be a divorce. I had made the break, and although I knew that deep down somewhere in my husband's heart he did love me I realised that I could never go back to him. I was too afraid of him, and I could not put my children through anything like that ever again.

The divorce became very traumatic, and seemed never-ending, and, despite my fears of him following me, everything seemed to settle down. I was back in the house with the children and he was granted visiting rights and instructed to pay maintenance and after nearly three years all the horrors of the divorce were pretty much behind me. He came to take the children out on a couple of occasions and the maintenance payments stopped after only one week. Although I was very upset about the money, as times were very hard bringing up four children on my own, my heart went out to my children. They loved their father as any and every child does and children shouldn't be made to choose; they are, as I well know, always the innocent party.

I wanted to make amends to them, wanted so much to heal the wounds in their young lives because I didn't want them to grow up bitter and resentful. I wanted to teach them that life did dish out unpleasant things sometimes and that it didn't always go the way that they might wish it, but that, whatever happened, and wherever they were, I would always be there for them, that I would always have time for them, and love them for all eternity. I tried to teach them to stay on the straight and narrow and, although life would take them off this road probably more times than they could count, as long as they strived to get back on it, everything would be all right. I also taught them to love and care for each other, and to respect other people, and their wishes. I started to remember how sad and alone I had been all my childhood, and I didn't ever want my children to feel the same. I promised them that, God willing, I would always be there for them, not just while they were growing up, but forever.

I became a different person, or did I? After all those years of acting, being someone that I wasn't, I became myself again. I had to work to afford to bring up four children, and I can, on numerous occasions remember having to leave them in the care of Paul, the eldest, whilst I had to work but they worked hard for me, although they were children. We had this respect for each other; we would always help each other; they knocked on my bedroom door and I knocked on theirs. I remember sometimes when I was working, the night before, I would lay a huge piece of polythene on the lounge carpet, and bring in buckets of sand and water for them to play with their lorries and trucks and soldiers. I would always say that they could not go out and play until I got home, as I was afraid of accidents, and I always left a list of things not to touch. Sometimes I would work nights and keep them up late so they would sleep late, and when I got home I would find them all in the one bed, mine. Looking back now I know that they were not angels but I feel that they had enough respect for me, to know how far to go. I was happy.

Any spare time I had, we would always go off somewhere as a treat. It was a sort of thank-you for being good for me and one particular time stands out in my mind. I had heard that the Pope was visiting Cardiff City and after talking it over with the children, we decided that we would go and see him. I booked three days off work and made plans to spend the whole three days camping in the car. I had learnt to drive several years before my divorce, even though at the time it had caused a lot of bother. I persevered, and now I was very pleased that I had. I had an old estate car, very shabby looking, but a good runner although sometimes I could barely afford to put any petrol in it. Yet, when I only put a few pounds' worth in, it seemed to run for miles on fresh air.

We were all set, the whole car packed with bedding and food and the children had all to squeeze up together. I remember we were all very excited and as with most of our trips the weather was kind to us and shortly after we left home out came the sun. The drive to Cardiff took just over an hour, and we had decided on the way that we would stop and have a picnic lunch, and then have a look around the shops. One thing that stands out in my mind about my children is, that whatever I did for them, no matter how much or how little, it always brought a smile to all their faces and for me those smiles could light up the whole world.

I knew my way around Cardiff quite well, having brought the children there several times for the karate championships so we looked around the shops and had whatever treats we could afford before setting off to find the address of where the Pope was going to be, and camp out—that was our plan. Much to our surprise when we got to this huge field two days before the Pope was due, there was another carload of people who had decided to do exactly the same as us. We got quite friendly with this other family, and I was relieved that they were there as I wasn't too happy about spending the night in the car in what seemed to be the middle of nowhere. We had a picnic tea and afterwards the children played in the wooded area with strict instructions from me not to go too far. I found plenty to do, getting things ready for sleeping that night and eventually dusk came and we all bedded down in the back of the car. It was a bit squashy but more fun and we all giggled and took turns to tell the others to move over. We told jokes, played I-spy, fidgeted, argued and, eventually, fell asleep. I remember waking early, trying to find a small space to stretch my aching limbs which in turn woke the children. One by one, after a few moans and groans and wriggling into their clothes, we emerged from the car to a wonderful sunny day, birds singing, peace and tranquillity. We looked across to find that our new neighbours were still sleeping, all the windows in their vehicle still misted.

The next conversation was about how starving we all were, so, as a special treat, I suggested we drive into the centre and see if we could find a café, perhaps a working man's café, and have breakfast. We, surprisingly, found a café open quite quickly and we all piled in and I remember we had thick slices of toast and a hot drink and to us it was just like dining at the Ritz.

We were all very excited about seeing the Pope, and we decided to park the car back where we had stayed the night, as that's how far vehicles were allowed to go. Then we climbed over the stile and investigated the field where the Pope was going to give mass, we hoped, to crowds of people. When we got into the field we noticed that all the plots had been staked out, and the platform had been erected with steps leading to it for the Pope. I remember the children were dashing about choosing a place where we could be and as we were going to be second in the queue to get in we could choose a place right up at the front. The Pope was due at midday tomorrow but the grass hadn't been cut and stood almost two feet tall. We went back to the car and the other family that was there before us suggested that we should carry all our bedding and things up to the other field and camp by the stile as soon there would be a crowd of people and we would lose our place. This meant that we would have to sleep out in the open that night and the children found this really exciting but I had mixed feelings.

We secured the car and set off dragging and carrying, and stopping every five minutes to sort out the squabbling and to have a rest because, after all, Denis was only six years old. Although they squabbled from time to time, when it mattered they were always there for each other. For the rest of the day we played games, picked wild flowers and generally lounged about enjoying the sunshine. At about six-thirty that evening we noticed other people coming down the track towards the stile where we were, then within a few more hours the whole area was filled with people camping out in line behind us. Our friends were first in line, we were second, and we thought that was great, so we set out the bedding on the ground for our second night's sleep, this time out in the open. The ground was quite damp and after much chatting, and a lot of excitement from the crowds, we eventually settled down to sleep. Once again morning came, and we awoke this time feeling quite cold and damp, but, after a make-do breakfast of biscuits and lemonade and the excitement, we soon forgot the hardships. It wasn't long before we found out that the Pope's visit had been delayed and he was now scheduled to arrive at eight to eight-thirty that evening. We were, of course, all disappointed. We were running out of food and there was no way we could get through the crowds and get to the car without losing our place in the queue.

When the news got through that the Pope was going to be late the officials decided to take down the barriers and let the people in to the field and, like we had planned, we went through second and secured a place right at the front of the platform. I remember we laid all our bedding down to flatten the long grass which they still hadn't cut, the children diving on it. We didn't have proper waterproof covers, we only had the blankets from our beds at home and they were beginning to feel quite damp. The rest of the day seemed to go slowly and at about five o'clock that evening the children had crawled into the damp bedding and fallen asleep. They were completely worn out by this time and the field was completely full. I can only describe it as being like Glastonbury Festival. There were Red Cross officials, police and lots of people wearing fluorescent jackets directing the crowds pouring into the field. I remember two Red Cross officials came up to me and the children and asked how we were and they began to examine the children. One official looked at the other and said, 'We need to get these children out of here quickly, they are close to hypothermia,' then they looked at me and repeated what they had said to each other and asked me where I was from. I explained our mini-adventure to them, and they said for me to pack everything up, and they would get an ambulance to take us back to the car. I couldn't believe it, and although we would not be seeing the Pope, my first concern was my children's safety. The two officials put the children in the ambulance and I too clambered in with all our belongings. All our lovely bedding now looked like something from a derelict house. The ambulance slowly drove us out of the field and I often think how lucky we were to have been up at the front of the field because, had we been in the middle of the crowd, I don't think anyone would have noticed us, let alone been able to get us out, if they did. I dreaded to think what might have happened to the children.

As we were driven away from the crowds one of the officials was on his radio to the police who had arranged to meet us at the car. By now the children were all wide awake, feeling a bit groggy and disappointed that they wouldn't be seeing the Pope, but much more occupied with their present new adventure. After a lot of weaving in and out of the crowd, the ambulance eventually got us to the car where two policemen were waiting for us. As I stepped out of the ambulance, I was amazed to see that there were still crowds of people pouring down this track road to get a glimpse of the Pope or, more so, I suspected, to receive his blessing from the mass. At that precise moment I felt that we had already received ours, by being found by the Red Cross and brought to safety. Looking back, I shudder to think what may have happened had they not discovered the children when they did and I only have the fullest admiration for them. After we had all settled in the car, and said our thank-yous to the ambulance men who in my book deserve a medal for getting us through that crowd, the police asked us to follow them, saying they would escort us back on to the motorway. They said that I should go straight home, give the children a hot bath, a hot drink and put them to bed. The police gave us an escort most of the way out of Cardiff, slowly taking us through the crowds and the children were all so excited, watching the blue flashing light, and we were laughing and joking and wondering if this was what it was like to be a pop star, or royalty, and then one of them said, 'I expect the people think we are really important.' Then another said, 'What? In this car?' and we would all fall about laughing; even then we were still on our adventure. The police waved us off onto the motorway, and we were on our way home. The children were still feeling a bit shivery and every now and again I could hear their teeth chattering, but, with all the reminiscing we did on the way home about our three days in Cardiff and cuddling up to each other, in just under an hour we were home. I remember when the children were all ready, warm and cosy, for bed, we looked at each other and could not believe that after all that endurance we never even got to see the Pope but we have the tickets to prove it. We certainly have the memories of what nearly was, but wasn't.

Before I fell asleep myself that night I lay for a while thinking how much I loved doing things with my children and of always loving them, and needing them, and that was what made my life complete.

We had had numerous adventures like our 'papal visit'. Whenever I could get a few days off work and I had a couple of pounds to spare, we would be off somewhere. Whether the seaside, picnicking, or just for a ramble through the fields, blackberrying, what made all these trips so special was the fact that, wherever we went or whatever we did, we always did everything together. Sometimes Sean would have piles of papers to deliver at the weekend to gain some pocket money, and if we planned to go off somewhere, we would all get up early, and deliver the papers with Sean, everything with them being team work. I did, as all mothers do, have some hair-raising experiences with them such as Sean breaking both his arms swinging from a rope hanging from a tree, Wendy having her thumb lanced, Denis breaking his arm and the doctor taking off the plaster and cutting his arm quite badly. Of course, along with the usual knocks and falls, was the hidden worry of Paul's heart murmur.

CHAPTER
TWELVE

I was now forty years of age, and as the saying goes, 'Life begins at forty'. It certainly took on some big changes for me. I had been taking the children to karate classes for nearly three years and during the last year I had taken up karate myself. Whilst at the leisure centre one evening, one of the other contestants approached me and asked if I was still on my own with four children, and, if so, would I be interested in meeting a friend of his? He was also divorced with children and this person went on to say that he thought his friend and I would be a perfect match. I immediately put up my guard and replied, 'No thank you,' and 'I don't need to meet anyone, thank you,' and walked away. I couldn't bear the thought of anyone spoiling the happiness I now had. I remember that I had asked the children one time when we were all sat at the table together having tea, 'How would you feel if I met somebody else?' and a very quick response came from Paul, 'I would hate him,' he said. I went on to say that I hadn't met anybody yet, so how could he hate 'nobody' and he replied, 'I would just hate him anyway,' and it wasn't discussed any more.

Much to my annoyance at the time, this person brought his friend to the karate class three weeks later and promptly walked up to me and said, 'This is Sue, and this is Dave,' and then just as quickly walked away again and left us both, mouth agape, with each other. Being caught unawares made me more annoyed, and I decided to ignore this 'Dave person' in the hope that it would save him and me a lot of embarrassment and he would just go away, but he didn't. He politely asked me if I would like a drink, to which I replied with a curt, 'No thank you,' then he sat down beside me, and for the next hour at least neither of us spoke to each other.

My daughter then came out of her class and whispered to me, 'Who is that man?' and I told her the whole story and to my surprise she turned again to me and said, 'Oh go on, Mum, it will be nice for you to have someone, and you can't be mean to him, can you?' At that moment Dave got up and walked to his friend who had introduced us and apparently said to him, 'Well that was a dead loss. Could you take me home, please?' His friend came over to me again and explained how upset Dave was and would I just give him a chance and I still said no. Then he asked me for my phone number and said that he didn't want to be the negotiator and perhaps we could sort it out together. Very reluctantly I wrote down my phone number and handed it to him. On the way home I told my daughter, and she was very excited and of course there was the twenty questions. 'What if he rings you? What will you say? Will you go out with him?' And I remember that we both ended up giggling and totally going off into a dream world of world cruises and riches beyond our belief.

Shortly after I got home that evening, and before the children had gone to bed, the telephone rang and Wendy answered, then, holding her hand over the mouthpiece and grinning like a Cheshire cat she said, 'It's for you, Mum, it's that man from karate,' and she handed me the phone. For the first time for at least twenty years I felt like a teenage girl again, going on her first date.

'Hello,' I said, and a voice replied, 'This is Dave; we met under strained circumstances at your karate class this evening,' and before I could say a word he went on to say, 'I wonder if you would like to meet up with me one evening?'

I looked across the room and I could see my daughter jumping up and down making all sorts of signs at me. 'He wants to meet me,' I said to her and she nodded at me.

'Go on, Mum,' she said. I then agreed with Dave that I would meet him and I grabbed a pencil to write down instructions and his telephone number. All that was left to be decided was when. I said I would leave that to him, and after we had ping-ponged it back and forth for a while he suggested the next evening, at his house at seven-thirty. I had no idea where it was that I was supposed to go but told him I would find it, and we both said a very formal goodbye and put the phone down. My daughter came over and gave me a big hug she was so pleased for me and I glanced at the boys who were busying themselves with something to see what their reaction was. When I asked them what they thought about their mother going out on a date, 'Great' came their reply and they went on with what they were doing. I went into the kitchen to make a cup of tea and I began to daydream. I was about to meet someone and I had very mixed feelings, part fear, fear that all this happiness that I had found with the children would be tarnished and excitement, the excitement of feeling like a young girl again about to go on her first date. The shout of 'Mum, can we have a drink please?' soon brought me back to reality and after looking at the time I realised it was way past their bedtime.

Before I went to bed myself that night I took time to think about what I was about to do. I reminded myself that I was happy, with the children, that we all went to karate classes twice a week, sometimes three times and I met lots of people there just for company. I think I even had a secret crush on the karate instructor, which I knew nothing could come of, as he was married with a lovely family. My life was good and I was enjoying it and I asked myself the question, 'Should I change it?' I remember ringing my best friend who lived very near to us and was a wonderful friend to me and always there for me, and an extremely good listener.

'Hello Pat,' I said. 'Guess what?'

She knew the minute she heard my voice that it was me and said, 'What have you done now?' and I started to tell her that I had been introduced to this man at karate classes and that he had telephoned me when I got home from classes, and asked me out on a date and that I had arranged to meet him at his house tomorrow evening, at seven-thirty. She stopped me before I could say any more, 'Oh my God, Sue,' she said, 'You can't just go to a strange man's house—he might be Jack the Ripper. Ring him back and tell him you will meet him somewhere else,' so I agreed, and she went on to say, 'And when you get home after the date, ring me to let me know you are home safe.' She said she would wait up and that it didn't matter what time it was. That's the kind of friend she was. Pat was married with two sons, similar ages to my boys and they all went to the same Catholic school about a half hour's walk away. When the children were small, we would take turns in the car to take them to school and fortunately her husband was a very understanding man and would leave us at times nattering for hours. If I had any worries about anything at all I always knew that I could go to Pat; she was always there for me.

After promising her that I would ring her the next night as she had asked, I said goodnight and put the phone down. After mustering enough courage, I rang Dave back and said it might be best if I met him somewhere else, and he readily agreed and I felt that he was afraid that I was going to change my mind and that he would have agreed to anything that I suggested. Eventually he agreed to meet outside his local pub. It was January, very dark and miserable weather, and he asked how he would recognise me, and I remember making a joke and saying, 'You will hear me before you see me,' as I had a real old car with an engine that sounded like a tractor. He gave a chuckle and we both said goodnight to each other, and 'see you tomorrow'.

Tomorrow came, the children went off to school as usual, and I went off to work. I was working at that time at a nursing home for the elderly as an auxiliary nurse and although it was very hard work I enjoyed it. It fitted in very well with having four children, the matron being very understanding and always happy to give me working shifts to fit in with my family. The children were always very supportive towards me if I got home late and they would help with everything at home, getting the tea, clearing up, Paul and Sean being older now and very capable of taking care of the younger ones for me. I always left them strict instructions, like I imagine most mothers do, not to answer the door to anyone, don't use the cooker, and no going outside to play while I was at work. Most of the time they were at school but if I was given an occasional awkward shift, I knew they would be there to help. I would explain to them that without my job there would be no treats, especially any extra hours I did because that money enabled us to go on trips and I jokingly would remind them of our 'papal visit' trip, and we would all roll about laughing.

Like all children, if there was a chance of staying up late they would try and seize it and that night they asked if they could wait up for me. I said no, that they had school the next day and that I would tell them everything in the morning. I remember them all waving to me from the window as I left to meet Dave and for a moment I thought, what am I doing? Why am I going? I am so happy as it is, but I continued to get into the car and I waved them out of sight.

I was never a very good navigator when I was driving, but eventually I found the place that I was meeting Dave. I was very much on time and as I pulled into the kerb I saw him waiting on the other side. I parked the car and, feeling very nervous, I walked towards him and we exchanged greetings and went into the pub for a drink. From the very first instant, Dave was a perfect gentleman, he too being nervous and after I had had time to realise that he was on his best behaviour I took a chance, and went back to his house thinking all the time what my best friend, Pat, had said. I remember the date went well and we talked of our differences and our children. Dave had three sons, one married, one at university and the other, a fourteen-year-old living at home with him. I remember we got on really well right from the start and I told him towards the end of the evening what Pat had said to me, and he laughed and said, 'She must be a good friend to care so much.'

I enjoyed Dave's company that night; he had worked hard at making everything just right for me—a little wine, soft music—and I felt very relaxed. At the end of the date he walked me to the car, parked at the rear of his house, and we kissed goodbye, and then he hurriedly asked if he could see me again. It seemed that if he didn't ask quickly I would change into a pumpkin. I said yes, that I would see him again, but reminded him that I had four children, and that there was no way in this world that I would involve them in anything that might hurt them. He said he understood, and that he liked me so much could he see me the next night? I agreed, we made the arrangements, and we once again said goodnight to each other. Shivering and teeth chattering, I got in the car, waved goodbye and drove home.

I was like an excited teenager and after one date I had decided that I liked Dave very much. I remember telling the children before they left for school the next morning but the boys just seemed to shrug their shoulders. I didn't over-react with them. I didn't want them ever to feel pushed out. My daughter seemed as excited as I was. 'What's he like, Mum? Where did you go?' Another twenty questions, but I loved her so much for it, to feel that, for such a young daughter, she was always so concerned for me. I told her how I had rang Auntie Pat, that's what the children called her, when I got home and how she was pleased for me also. Looking back now, although I was forty years of age, I was still acting out my missed childhood.

Dave and I did all the things that couples do together, we laughed, we cried, and we fell madly in love with each other, and he was a very caring and sincere person. We somehow managed to see each other every night since that first date and, after I had known him for a month, he asked to meet my children. He invited us all over for a Sunday evening for tea, and after the initial shyness and apprehension, everyone got on very well together.

I didn't lose my happiness with the children, we had so many good times, all of us together, and he was very good to my children, but always, very deep down inside my most inner thoughts, I kept thinking of my stepfather. I remembered how horrible he had been to me, and how he wouldn't let my mother love my brother and me, so I would always say to Dave that although I loved him very much, nothing, or nobody, would ever come between me and my family and he was always so generous in his acceptance of this. All those times in the past when I had ask myself over and over again why nobody loved me, why nobody cared, and all those horrible things that had happened to me—although they were still deep-seated in my mind, they didn't seem to matter any more.

For the first time in my life I felt like I had the best of both worlds. There were of course minor ups and downs, nothing serious—after all, the children were growing up, experiencing the usual teenage feelings, one day an adult, the next day a child. Paul had made friends with Dave's youngest son David, and they seemed to get on very well, which was the start of Paul growing up and leaving home. This I found very hard to accept as I had always kept them so close together as a family. Yet I kept reminding myself that I had met someone and I must allow them to do the same although it was hard to have to accept that I would have to let them grow up and lead their own lives. I convinced myself that if I had done a good job of bringing them up then they would always be respectful to their parents, and each other.

Dave was a wonderful person to them and although they didn't see much of their real father, they always remembered him on special occasions and, as they were growing up, each one of them in turn went to stay with him for a while. I always tried not to condemn him in front of them, as I knew that he was their natural father and always would be. I wanted them to make their own decisions and form their own opinions. It wasn't always easy, and at times I let myself down, but hopefully not enough to make a difference.

Eighteen months after we had met, Dave asked me to marry him and my first outward reaction was of excitement and I couldn't wait to tell the family, who by now had accepted Dave and were just as happy for me. My inner thoughts were fearful—fear of making another mistake, fear of going back to being unhappy because I couldn't bear that. I was happy now and I didn't want anything to change while we were a proper family, and had plenty of love around us, and I was so afraid of losing all that.

Despite my fears, I accepted Dave's proposal, and we were to be married in April. As with all wedding arrangements there was much to be organised—flowers, outfits, cars and invitations. Wendy was always so willing and helpful when there was anything to be organised. She was twelve years of age now, and the thought of having a whole new outfit was incredibly exciting for her. I wanted to make sure that I involved all the children as much as I could in all the planning and preparations, for I not only felt that it was going to be Dave's and my day but also theirs. We were a family and everyone was important. I remember when we sat down to make a guest list, I felt sad that Denise and Sean could not be there to celebrate with me, or dear Flo and her girls, and for a while I daydreamed: where were they now? And remembered that I had found happiness once before, during my three-year stay in Dublin and although my marriage didn't work out I had made some good friends there. I remembered Ma, how kind she was to me, and how sad that a marriage break-up could change that kindness and although I understood the reasons I didn't want to accept them.

I could feel tears in my eyes, then I was brought back to reality by Wendy saying, 'What's the matter, Mum?' And hugging her closely to me, I replied, 'Nothing, darling, just Mum going down memory lane.' She would always say, 'Tell me, Mum, tell me all about when you were young like me.' Then I would sit and tell her all about my parents sending me and my brother away to Australia, and how I would always love her so much that I would never let anything hurt her or bring her sadness; that I would always be there for her and the boys. We would hug each other until we nearly crushed each other's bones. We made out the list, my brothers and sisters, their husbands and children, Dave's family—his mother like mine had died, and I remember saying to him on one occasion how sad it was that our mothers could not be there to see how happy we were. He had had a difficult childhood, and his mother had suffered in silence much the same as mine had. Yet, while somehow I always managed to accept all the sadness in my life, Dave found his hard to come to terms with. Thank God we had found each other, and we always seemed to complement each other. I was a flighty spur-of-the-moment person and Dave a planner and a plodder, but his tolerance of me, and his adoration for me made me feel so happy. Sadly, he drifted from his own family, under strained circumstances, and made me his queen.

The lists, like all wedding lists, seemed endless, and after omitting a few very distant relatives, we drew the bottom line. I was looking forward to seeing all the family, but especially Roy and his new wife and family. It had been so long since we had seen each other, and ages since we had spoken to each other. Life had just drifted on by and I had found happiness and I hoped that he had also found happiness. I remember thinking about his first marriage and how I had travelled from Dublin to be there and how happy I was for him, and I began to think how strange that both our marriages had failed. For a few seconds I felt that feeling of fear override my happiness.

The night before my wedding to Dave was a nightmare. Weeks before I had spent a night out with my sisters and some friends and Dave had enjoyed a night out with his friends from work. Reminding Dave that I had two brothers-in-law and two brothers, I suggested that he should get to know them better and arrange a night out with them, just a few drinks and a chat. This he did, but only one brother-in-law and my youngest brother could attend, and they decided to go out the night before Dave and I were to be married. I had plenty to do that evening, getting all the children bathed and to bed early, and making sure the flowers that were lying all over the lounge floor were kept watered and fresh, so I encouraged him to go out and off he went. I busied myself all evening, until finally everything was ready. I remember it was midnight, and Dave and I were getting married at ten o'clock in the morning at the registrar office in town so I thought that I would sit down with a cup of tea and then get myself off to bed ready for the big day.

I sat on the settee. The room was still, all the flowers lay in front of me, and I began to think. My first thoughts were of Denise; my baby had died in this room. I could suddenly see all the upturned furniture that my first husband had smashed, and then recalled the telegram, and Sean—how he had died came rushing back to me. Flo, where was she? She should be at my wedding. My stepfather was giving me away, where was my mother? I was asking myself horrible questions; why did he live and she have to die? Why did all those people I had loved die? The tears rolled down my face and soon turned into loud sobbing and I remember making myself cry more and more by thinking about all my past life right back to when I was a small child. Where were all my friends that had been in the children's home with me? I kept looking at the flowers on the floor; they looked all blurry now as my eyes were so full of tears.

'Where are you?' I said out loud, meaning Dave, and suddenly I felt so alone. I knew the children were upstairs in bed asleep, so, still looking at the flowers, I shouted out loud again, 'Why am I getting married again? I don't want to be married. I hate all men.' I wanted to get up and screw all the flowers up until there was nothing left of them but I couldn't. I somehow felt stuck to the settee, unable to move. I looked at the clock; he was hours late, and had no key, so I had to wait up to let him in. As I waited all this bitterness and resentment was building up in me, as if all my whole forty years of living was going to explode inwardly. I could see in my mind all these people with no faces all grabbing bits of me. It was so frightening at one stage I remember thinking that I was going mad and I began walking up and down the room, talking out loud.

Where was he, I kept repeating over and over? It was almost as though I was working myself into a frenzy, when suddenly I heard a tap on the window and I stormed to the front door, opened it and saw Dave standing there, smiling. I said, 'Where the bloody hell have you been? Get in.' He looked puzzled and walked past me to go into the lounge and I remember screeching at him all sorts of abuse. I knew what I was doing; I knew that I didn't want to do it, but I couldn't stop myself. He asked if I would like a cup of tea, and walked towards the kitchen, so I took off my shoe and flung it the whole length of the room at him. 'Don't walk away from me when I'm talking to you,' I yelled and I could see that he was confused.

He didn't want to provoke me; he didn't want to say or ask me anything. At one stage he said, 'Come on, let's go to bed; we're getting married tomorrow.'

'Getting married?' I said. 'I don't want to marry you, I don't want to get married ever again.'

He looked at me and said he was going to bed and I remember barricading the doorway with my body. 'Oh no you're not,' I said, and I began to question him about where he had been that night, and why was he so late. Why hadn't he taken a key?

Everything I could possibly think of asking, I asked, and he must have reached the stage when he could take no more and he looked up and said, 'Right, I'm leaving,' and very calmly he asked me to let him through the door.

I immediately responded with, 'Where do you think you are going? Don't you dare leave! You're marrying me in the morning, you're not going to make a fool of me.' Such to-ing and fro-ing went on all night until seven-thirty in the morning. My face was like a red tomato swollen from crying. Dave had sort of calmed me down by now, and we walked up the stairs and went to bed, knowing that in half an hour's time his father would be calling around to help me with the children and have breakfast with us. I remember Dave and I lying beside each other in bed and I slid my hand over his and we held hands really tightly. I kept thinking how he must hate me and that he must be wondering what on earth he was about to marry.

We did get married that day, and everything was wonderful and, looking back now, I can only explain my outburst as fear,

fear of reliving my past, fear of losing my children, fear of the unknown. That outburst of mine was my way of cleansing myself and although I had no secrets from Dave I somehow needed to let all the hatred and sadness out.

CHAPTER THIRTEEN

Very soon I found all this behind me. I was happy and we were planning a trip to Canada. Dave had a brother living there and of course my eldest brother, Alan, had moved out there soon after he was married. I had kept in touch by letter occasionally but we didn't really know each other, not as brother and sister. Several times he had written and asked us to visit. Dave had sold 'his' house and we were living in 'mine' at that time, and with the money he had promised to take us to Canada. He knew I always wanted to see my eldest brother. I had spoken to Roy only briefly at the wedding; his new wife had not been too receptive. Roy and I had drifted so far apart for so many years now, I didn't really know him any more—and now I was about to get to know Alan. Although I was wonderfully happy, somehow I always seemed to be searching for something, or someone—I can't explain, I just couldn't let go. The children were of course excited about going to Canada and we had booked for a three-week stay, so there was much to do. After meeting Dave I had changed my job, and I was now working in a day centre looking after the elderly, which I enjoyed very much and when Dave had time off work he would come and help me. We were like two lovebirds, never apart unless we had to be, always doing everything together and life was happy for all of us. There were the usual family disagreements. Paul was seventeen now and had gone to live with his father which at the time had devastated me, but we had had an argument and in a temper I had said to him, 'Pack your bags and go and live with your father, you're just like him.' So he did. Fortunately his father only lived a few minutes' drive away, so I got to see Paul two or three times a week. I had to accept the fact that he was growing up and making his own way in life.

Dave's son, David, had also lived with us for a while, and had become very best mates with Paul, which, sadly, left Sean out, and although he didn't say anything at the time, in later years it came out in conversation. I have to admit I found young David very hard to get on with, as he had been given complete freedom by his father, Dave, before we met. He had been back and forth, living with his mother, then his father and, most of the time, he was very resentful of his father remarrying. I think now that having to share with four other children was very hard for him, especially as he had been used to having all his own way. Dave's divorce had been quite traumatic for him and his boys, although the elder two were away from home. David had been on his own for three years with his father and had been spoilt with material things but in my mind he had not had very much love. There was a distinct divide between them, and sadly that's the way it always was and still is now. Yet Dave made a wonderful stepfather for my children and I do believe that he loves them as his own although I must take some of the credit for the way I always worked hard at keeping us together.

We had booked with Wardair Airlines and, after crossing the days off the calendar one by one, the date of departure had arrived and I remember it was a cold, wet and windy, middle-of-June day. Sean, Wendy, Denis, Dave and I were all set to go. Paul was still living with his father and, feeling all grown up now, didn't want to go on a family holiday. This of course upset me; splitting the family up was very hard for me to accept and I had to keep reminding myself that one by one they were growing up, and Paul was first.

The taxi arrived to take us to the coach depot, which would take us to the airport. I was still deciding whether to wear coats or pack them. In the end I decided to do neither. The suitcases were already at bulging point; carrying coats would be a bind and I was pretty sure that when we arrived at Toronto the climate would be much warmer than here. The coach trip was very short to Cardiff airport, and of course the mention of Cardiff to the children brought back some chuckles for our papal visit that nearly was. It was all we could do to keep the children occupied, they were so excited. Dave and I had decided earlier that this was to be a trip of a lifetime, and we had promised each other not to hassle the children—just let them have a long lead, so to speak, because we wanted everyone to enjoy themselves.

When we all boarded the plane, we were flabbergasted at the sheer size of it; it was absolutely huge. I was a little but not too nervous at the thought of flying. I didn't want to scare the children so we all settled into our seat with the children fidgeting for some time before they really got settled. Dave and I were biting our tongues, trying not to yell at them, and eventually they did settle down as all the passengers did and we were ready for take-off.

Wow, it was fantastic. There was so much for the children to do and the air hostesses gave them so much attention, always making sure they were occupied and that also applied to the adults. All our meals were served on china dishes and plates and superbly presented, and we felt as though we had booked first class. The flight lasted eight hours and flying into Toronto Airport was breathtaking. Everything looked so big, and the climate was so warm. I was wearing a royal blue warm dress, and soon began to feel uncomfortable, Dave was in a nice cream suit so he very much looked the part and was able to take off his jacket to keep cool. The children were dressed for an English summer and all the time we were struggling to get through the airport procedures they would keep repeating over and over, 'Isn't it hot?' But we all felt good and agreed that this was going to be a holiday of a lifetime. My brother Alan and his wife Valerie were there to meet us and at first I thought I wouldn't recognise him although he had travelled several times to the UK on holidays I only ever got to see him for a few minutes. He always seemed to be in a rush and would apologise for not being able to spend more time with me then rush off to visit somewhere else. I remember I used to get upset and say to myself that I was his sister and would think that he would want to see me the most. All those years had gone by and I hardly knew my own brother but now I was about to spend three whole weeks with him. I remember hugging him at the airport with a feeling of 'never ever let me go'. Dave had borrowed a very good camera from his company's photographic department, to make sure we would have lots of photographs to look back on in the years ahead, and he carefully took photos of the first meetings and the farewells, and all the three weeks in between.

We drove to Midland, where my brother and family lived; it only seemed like a few minutes away as once we were outside the city the roads were quiet and straight, and the driving much easier and more relaxing. The house was very large and, like most Canadian houses, there was a basement which was the same size as the level above, so the children could relax in their own space along with their two cousins, Rob and Drew. Rob and Drew were older, aged seventeen and nineteen which was ideal as they were able to look after our three children. Sean celebrated his fifteenth birthday in Canada, and we all had a really good time. Alan and Valerie also owned a holiday cottage on an island so we spent several days there. It was fabulous—fishing, canoeing, relaxing in the warm sunshine—and the children loved the freedom. They especially liked it when Rob would turn up in his small motor boat and take them to the mainland. My children would spend time with Rob and Drew during their time off from their summer holiday jobs on release from college.

There was, as with most wonderful things, one nightmare and that was the insects. Dave and I were eaten alive, and apparently June and July were the worst months in Canada for mosquitoes. We would lie in bed at night and pray that they would leave us alone. Dave had lumps on his face the size of hard-boiled eggs, swollen and bleeding from his constant scratching. I had a slightly different problem and I was soon to find out that I was allergic to mosquito bites, and several parts of my body began to swell seriously enough for Alan to call a doctor who prescribed special cream. After a few very uncomfortable days of not being able to walk I soon got back into the swing of things again. The children oddly enough never had a single bite and the reason for this still remains a mystery.

It did turn out to be a holiday of a lifetime as we went everywhere and did almost everything. Alan was determined to give his only sister and her family a wonderful experience and cost and time knew no boundaries.

We visited the Indian encampment at Penetanguishene, the Blue Mountain ski run, Safari Parks, and Rob and Drew took the children to the Canadian Disney World. We visited friends of theirs and were made so welcome, I couldn't believe that life could be like this. We went up in the CN Tower—that was an indescribable experience. All these things were amazing, wonderful and fabulous, but Niagara Falls was sensational, there being no words to describe the feeling, the wonder, and the sheer size of the falls. I remember we were all dressed in bright yellow raincoats and hats, souwester style, and we walked down several steps and came out on a balcony actually under the falls, and we could reach out and touch the water cascading down at such an incredible force. The memory of Niagara Falls will stay with me forever as I am sure it will for Dave and the children. During the second week of our holiday, Alan allowed us use of the car to travel to a small town called Zurich to visit Dave's brother and family. We stayed a glorious week with them. They lived and worked on a farm and the children helped with the animals and Wendy enjoyed lots of horse riding. We spent time on the beach and the whole week was very welcoming and relaxing. As the saying goes, all good things come to an end and so did our three-week Canadian holiday. Sadly we said our goodbyes at the airport and I was left alone with Alan for a few minutes and I hugged him again. I remember saying to him that I felt that he had crammed the forty years that I had missed out having him for a brother into three weeks. I told him that I would never forget this wonderful experience and I kissed him on the cheek one more time and waved him and his family goodbye.

We carried home with us some wonderful memories and as I fastened my seat belt for take-off I said a small prayer thanking God for making me so happy and asking Sean and Denise to guide us all home safely.

Our journey home was very similar to our outward flight, and we arrived back home, tired, weary and sad that it was all over, but so happy and grateful to have had the experience and all the photos and memories to go with it. I felt sure as the children grew older they would experience many exciting places of travel, but Canada will always hold a special place in their hearts. I know it does in mine.

One of the nicest things about being a complete family was that we always sat around the table to discuss any envisaged changes, or anything that the children might want to do. In fact, we would sit around the table lots of times, especially after meal times. Dave would ask general-knowledge questions and as soon as anyone got three right they could leave the table and, to make it fair, that included me. As everyone enjoyed it so much, it became a family ritual and even when their friends called they would join in and sometimes we would still be at the table at ten o'clock in the evening. That wasn't because nobody could get three questions right! It was because Dave would make it so interesting for them, so they enjoyed it as a learning exercise. It has always held them in good stead and became a private family joke. We might all be out somewhere together and one would shout out, 'Name the five great lakes, Wendy,' or 'How do you spell giraffe, Denis?'

This particular night we were all sat around the table for a different reason. Dave and I had talked about moving house; he had sold his house and we were all living in what was deemed to be my house since my divorce and we thought it would be nice to have a house that could be 'our house'. Thus we had decided to ask the children to see how they would respond. We asked, and they responded, not very well at first, but we had expected that because, after all, this was their home and maybe they would have to change schools, change friends and so on. So we put to them all the fors and againsts we could possibly think of and after long discussion we decided to look around at the market prices and see what was on offer. We spent most of our free time house hunting and in the meantime we had put my house on the market for sale. Houses were quite expensive at the time, and we were obviously keen on making a few pounds if possible during the selling and buying. We had had some nice days out in South Wales and thought we might look at the house prices just over the Severn Bridge, which is what we did. We chose a lovely bungalow, the usual three-bedroomed type, but with really nice big gardens, and as we both enjoyed gardening we fell in love with it. After telling the children at the weekend, we took them to see it.

Their first reaction was terrible; they hated it. They sulked, cried and I remember Dave saying, 'We are the parents; we have decided that children don't always get their own way.' I was taken aback and as always very much on the defence regarding my children, so suggested that we discussed it more fully when we got home. The thought of moving into this bungalow in Wales didn't go down too well. Wendy said it was too squashy and by that I took it that she meant too small, Denis didn't seem to mind either way; it was just another new adventure to him, and Sean was his usual quiet self. So I spoke to them one by one trying to find out their true feelings and each one of them said to me, 'As long as you are happy, Mum, then we're happy.'

That evening we were all sat watching television and I was reading the houses for sale column in the evening paper, and I spotted an advertisement that said 'four-bedroom detached house for sale, brand new, fully fitted carpets, unusual design, last one hence give-away price £45,000. Tel...' etc.

First, I read it again as Dave always said I jumped the gun at everything. 'Read the small print,' he would say. 'Always read the small print on everything.' So I did read it again and again until I could hold my tongue no longer. 'Hey everyone,' I said, 'listen to this,' and I read out the advert. The house was also in Wales in a small village. The children's response was the same as mine: 'Let's go and see it,' they said.

Dave who was a planner and a plodder sat there very undisturbed and calmly said, 'I thought we had already chosen a house, the bungalow.'

I glanced at the children and caught Wendy pulling a face, so I quickly said, 'Well we could go and see it—it's not far from the bungalow.'

In fact, it was a further four miles on. It was decided that I ring in the morning and go and see it. We had got a viewing the very same day and I allowed the children a day off school and set off for a day out. I think we had made up our minds to buy this house before we had even seen it and when we saw it there was no doubt whatsoever. Even Dave fell in love with it—it was beautiful. All new, beautifully carpeted throughout, large bedrooms with garden views and even a balcony on the master bedroom. The whole house was so spacious and a real bargain; houses like this in the city where we lived were twice this price. The children were dashing around choosing their bedrooms, Wendy was doing cartwheels on the spacious lounge floor and I could hear them saying that they would put this here and that there, and I knew then that this was to be our new family home.

The house was in a very small village, just five miles over the Severn crossing and we drove around and checked out the local schools and everything just seemed to fit into place perfectly. We had stopped off to have a drink and something to eat and I took time out just to stand and gather my thoughts. I had come a long way since my childhood and all those difficult years that followed, and now for just one split second I told myself that life was good, and maybe life did begin at forty. It certainly looked that way for me. I thought of Paul, who was still living with his father. I was seeing him regularly and he always spent time with his brothers and sister. I thought of how time was moving forward and around his eighteenth birthday the hospital would be calling on him to perform his heart operation. All these thoughts were rushing through my mind, and as always I would look up towards the sky and feel that Denise and Sean were watching over us.

Selling our house and buying this new one wasn't all plain sailing. We had had several prospective buyers for ours. I remember the first one in particular. A young couple came to view, and at the viewing they were quite taken with Dave's aquarium, which led to a lengthy conversation on the dos and don'ts of looking after fish. Having finished viewing the house, they said they liked what they saw, and would possibly be in touch. But the next morning when we all came downstairs for breakfast every single fish in Dave's aquarium had died and was floating on the top of the tank. It was dreadful; we were completely baffled as to how this could have happened, and why. I began to get a bit edgy about selling the house, thinking it was an omen. As my daughter, Denise, had died in this house, I started to believe that it was her way of saying, 'Please don't go.' Dave, being very understanding, said I was being silly and not to think like that, so I tried to put it out of my mind.

After a while and a few more viewings, things seemed to be going all right. We then, out of the blue, got a firm offer, a cash offer, no chain, outright purchase. A young family with three young children had been left money in a trust and after seeing our house they wanted to use the trust money to buy it. Everything was going well; we had purchased the new house with a hefty bridging loan, as there were others interested, and we were afraid of losing it. We had gone out on a financial limb and were very anxious to sell. Anxious to sell was an understatement—we were desperate! The bridging loan was costing us an arm and a leg and was crippling us financially. This new cash offer was just what we needed. We proceeded to move out and settle into our new home. The children were excited, although a little nervous of changing schools. Wendy and Denis found it easier but for Sean it was much harder. He missed Paul and wanted to grow up fast so he could do the things that he imagined Paul was doing. I knew this because one time he had asked me if he could he go and live with his father. I had said at the time that he was a little bit too young and maybe he could when he was older. I remember feeling frightened, frightened that my family was splitting up—what would I do without them? I began to panic, but brought myself back to my senses by reminding myself that my family wasn't splitting up, just growing up. That it was perfectly natural for the children to want to know their own father. But I knew I was right about one thing. Sean had to wait until he was a little older.

The changing of schools and making new friends was, I knew, very difficult for the children, but I was proud of them and they handled it extremely well. We had now completed our move to our new house.

My house we had left empty, as it was to be another two weeks to contract-signing. I remember it being the month of December and apart from the excitement we had wanted to move to the new house for Christmas. We had left the central heating on very low in my house just to keep the house from becoming damp and cold. We had to be careful because we couldn't afford to have heavy heating bills and we knew that we would have to pull in our belts for a while but we felt the new house was worth it.

House sales take on average about six to eight weeks to complete but ours was taking a little longer as the new buyers had been left the money in a trust. It was on the advice of this trust that they arranged a full survey to take place on my house. All these things took time, dragging on and on, but eventually we were on the final week before exchanging contracts. I had been over to the house weekly, just checking that everything was all right as an empty house could have been a target for vandals or break-ins.

I remember it being a Saturday morning when we intended going shopping. I had suggested to Dave that we travel over the bridge and check the house as contracts were being exchanged on the following Monday, then we could go shopping, before heading for home. Wendy was seeing her friend but Sean was staying in and had offered to look after Denis for us. Pulling up outside my 'old' house was quite emotional for me. I had spent eighteen years of my life there and there had been good times and bad times, and very sad times. Paul was born in this house; all my children were brought up in this house; my daughter Denise had died in this house and this was to be the last time I would go inside it. I turned the key in the lock, pushed open the front door, to be greeted with one of the worst nightmares of my life. Water, everywhere, water! It was literally cascading down the staircase. We rushed upstairs only to find that it was pouring from the loft hatch and we just stood there for a few seconds and looked at each other. Then I burst into tears. I don't think anybody could believe what it was like as we went into the back bedroom that used to be Sean's and found it was almost two inches deep in water. The door to what used to be our bedroom, which was directly under the loft hatch, had been completely stripped of its paint; the whole frame was now bare wood and all the paint strippings were on the floor. It was exactly the same downstairs as the lounge door was directly under the one above. In the lounge there was a bubble in the ceiling—the size of a car—just four feet from the floor level, full of water. I can only describe it as a giant cow's udder hanging from the ceiling. There was of course a telephone still connected in the house, ready to pass on to the new owner and I suddenly thought, 'Oh my God, will there be a new owner?' Just two days to signing contracts. I couldn't bear to think. The tears still rolling down my face as I shouted to Dave, 'What shall we do?'

Dave had established that there was a burst pipe in the loft, due to the cold weather and he said he thought it had been leaking for at least a week. I remember he tried to phone for a plumber and how it turned out to be an impossible task. Every plumber in the book was tied up as we had had some severe weather, and obviously other people were suffering the same problem. He decided to ring his work and luckily enough they contacted their site plumber and promised he would be with us as soon as possible. At that time, Dave had told me to go home and not to worry—that he would sort everything out. Yet I couldn't because I knew there was so much drying out to do, and repainting. I looked around for rags, or a bucket, but there was nothing—we had moved everything. I decided to drive to my young sister's house, only a mile away, and she gave me all the things I needed and an offer of help if I needed it. Dave had also rung the tool hire shop to hire a vacuum to suck up the water so I collected that too. I was so frantic that all this seemed to be organised in about five minutes. When I got back to the house with all the mopping-up equipment, the plumber was in the loft fixing the leaking pipe. He too was amazed at what he saw when he arrived, saying that he had never seen anything like it but when we explained that we hadn't visited the house for nearly a week he could then understand why there was so much water. A burst pipe going for twenty-four hours a day for a whole week—it's surprising how much water that is. By now, we had the suction vacuum going and I was mopping up where I could. Then we put the heating up to the highest level, hoping to dry out the carpets. I also set about wiping and drying down the woodwork, ready to put a coat of paint on. There was no time for undercoat. I had bought a brush and a tin of gloss and that would have to do.

The plumber, before he left, burst the bubble in the ceiling downstairs, and explained how it would just shrink back into place, explaining that the aertex on the ceiling was very strong and that we were lucky the whole ceiling hadn't come down. I remember thinking I was glad he thought we were lucky but it was incredible to watch this huge bubble, now leaking water from a few pin holes, gradually shrinking back towards the ceiling. We had rung the children and explained that we would be late home and to remind them to be careful on their own. Sean was always very good at taking charge and said he would make the tea, telling us not to worry as he would look after the others.

I remember it took us hours and hours and we were exhausted, and after painting where necessary and vacuuming the carpets until they were nearly worn out we stood back to admire our work to see if it would stand close inspection by the new owners and I couldn't believe it. Except for the windows all being steamed up from the wet, the heating on full, and the whole house like a sauna, we could see no clues to our disaster, not even the bubble that had shrunk back to the ceiling. If you looked really closely at it you could just see a very faint water mark. We were very proud of ourselves and exhausted. We also felt a little fraudulent not telling the new owners but, financial needs must, and that's the way it had to be. They signed the following Monday and as far as I know they are still in the house and that was over fourteen years ago. I still believed to this day that something or someone was telling me not to sell that house and I have always promised myself that if I ever win any money or get into a position where I could possibly buy that house back, I will, for my children.

CHAPTER FOURTEEN

Life got back to normal quite quickly and we carried on with our lives. We were enjoying our new home and the children had settled very well in their new schools and made lots of new friends, when I received a phone call from Paul. This wasn't unusual, as we were always in touch, although he wasn't living with us or for that matter with his father any more. He had rented a flat but was still my son and I loved him and worried about him just as much as the others. But this particular phone call was different. He went on to tell me that he had received a letter to say he had to go into hospital for his heart operation and I remember he was angry on the phone; he didn't want to go. He was a few months off his eighteenth birthday, feeling well and enjoying his life so I could understand the way he felt. Although it was an awful shock for me that the time had now arrived after all those years, I didn't want to let on to Paul that I was at all worried for fear of him not having it done. Heaven knows what the long-term effect might be if he made that decision. I told him that I would of course go with him and that I would collect him on the day, which I did.

The first two days of his being in hospital were for tests designed to make sure he was well enough to have the operation. The hospital staff agreed that he wasn't well enough as he had a slight cold about him so they sent him home. Then they called him again, two weeks later, then after two days they sent him home again saying that there was a virus going around in the hospital and that the wards had to be disinfected before any more operations could take place. All this had a serious effect on Paul, because he had not wanted the operation in the first place and now all this messing about only made him feel worse. He had rang me and said he wasn't going to bother and this was very worrying for me. I asked the surgeon the seriousness of his decision. Paul very reluctantly met me and we both went to see the surgeon and after waiting for quite a while in the waiting room Paul became more and more agitated. Eventually his name was called and we went in.

The surgeon looked at his notes, then looking directly at Paul then said, 'If you don't have this operation now, you will be on your back at the age of thirty, looking for a heart swap. Your liver will pack up and so will your kidneys. If you have this operation you will suffer slight discomfort for a few days.' He went on to say that it was a complicated operation but that he had performed many of them and his exact words to Paul were as before; 'It will be just like mending a bicycle puncture.' He then added, 'So stop wasting my time and have the operation.' I remember Paul looking at me and saying in a sort of mumbling voice, 'Oh all right then.' On the way home I wanted to hug him. I could understand how he felt and I was so afraid for him but I couldn't show him this for fear of upsetting him.

His next appointment came through a few weeks later with the all-clear from the hospital explaining that all operations were back on schedule and would Paul please come in for his tests. So, for the third time, which would unnerve anyone, Paul went into hospital. This time his tests were all clear and I was informed that they would carry out his operation the following morning at eight o'clock and I felt a shudder go through my body, wondering if I felt like that, how must Paul feel? Before I left to go home that night I tried to say all the right things to Paul and I hugged him and didn't want to let him go but he kept saying that he would be all right and for me not to worry. Those famous words 'don't worry' but this time they were not for me they were for Paul. I looked at him and I said, 'I love you, Paul, I love you with all my heart and soul and you are going to be all right, your Uncle Sean and your sister Denise will watch over you, so don't worry. I'll be here first thing in the morning.' As I walked off the ward, waving Paul out of sight, I prayed like I have never prayed before. 'Please God, don't take him from me.'

I remember lying awake most of the night wondering how Paul was feeling. Although the nurses had reassured me that they would give him something to help him sleep, I still felt that I wanted to be there beside him and I remember how endless that night seemed. Dave came with me to the hospital that morning and I remember the nurses saying there was nothing I could do. The doctor said the operation would take about eight hours and advised us to come back later. We went into town, had a coffee, and wandered around the streets. I felt like a fish out of water and said that I would rather be back in the hospital so we went back to the waiting room and waited, and waited.

One-thirty, and I asked the nurse how everything was and I will always remember her words. 'Just give me fifteen minutes to get him ready and you can come in.'

I jumped up and said, 'Is he all right?'

'He's fine,' the nurse said. 'Fifteen minutes, all right.' I felt like the whole world had been lifted from my shoulders and I felt the tears swell up into my eyes and I said over and over under my breath, 'Thank you God, thank you Sean and Denise.'

I was sitting by the side of his bed, holding his hand while he was still asleep from the anaesthetic. 'Paul, Paul,' I repeated over and over and within a few minutes he opened his eyes looked at me, and said, 'Hello Mum.'

My feelings at that precise moment were so wonderful. I can only describe them as being the same as the days each of my children were born, just as though all the black rain clouds had disappeared from my life and out had come the sun again.

Paul went straight into intensive care and, apart from hating being in hospital, he was making a very good recovery. We went in to see him two or three times a day and took the other children

161

in to see him and I was pleased that his real father had also gone in to see him. I had, naturally, told him about his son's operation, hoping for Paul's sake that he would visit. I remember we spoke briefly to each other in the hospital corridor about Paul and agreed that we were both relieved that he was recovering well and that everything about the operation was fine.

After a week Paul was to be discharged, and although he was nearly eighteen I pleaded with him to come back and stay with us for a while and, after much persuasion on our part, he agreed to stay for two weeks. I did understand his reasons because our new house was very far from his friends, but I felt that a couple of weeks' rest would do him good. I could look after him and spoil him silly while he was away from his fast-paced youthful life. The next two weeks went by very quickly, Paul very much back to normal and ready to go back to his flat and carry on with his life. He had a few instructions from the hospital concerning dos and don'ts such as: don't ride a bicycle for six weeks, don't lift anything heavy for six weeks, do try and live a normal life and do ring us, or your local doctor, if there are any worries. Of course there were also a million don'ts for me, his mother, but I was just so pleased to see him so well and that, after all these years of this 'cloud' hanging over him, it was all over. I was, of course, very reluctant to let him go again, but I knew that I must. He was now a grown man, making his own way in the world and, apart from a few minor ups and downs, a very capable young man who always made me feel proud.

Dave had agreed that the family deserved another holiday, it having been a busy year what with moving house and Paul's operation so we decided to all sit around the table and choose where we would like to go. After what seemed to be hours of discussion and nothing decided I asked, 'Why don't we go abroad like most families?' Dave had gone upstairs to fetch something and shouted down to me, 'Like where?' And I said, 'Well, somewhere like Spain.' 'Spain,' he shouted as he came back down the stairs, 'what has Spain got that this country hasn't got?' This conversation went on most of the evening and still nothing was decided. Morning came, and as usual the children went to school and Dave and I went off to work.

Later that day I received a telephone call from Dave. He often rang me at work so I wasn't surprised, until I answered when he said, 'I can't talk for too long, I'm busy. I just rang to tell you that I have just booked two weeks in Spain at a place called Denia. Never heard of it, but look at it this way. In four weeks it will be all over and we will be back home. Sorry, I can't talk now, bye darling, see you later.' And the phone went dead.

I felt like a small child that had just been given a big ice cream and I couldn't wait to tell the children and when I picked Dave up on the way home that evening I was still very excited.

The children were over the moon, Wendy so excited she almost wanted to start packing then and there. I remember they started to mark the days off the calendar, much as they had done when we had gone to Canada.

We were at the airport with some friends who had driven us and there was panic on Dave's face. 'What's wrong?' I asked.

'I can't find the tickets,' he replied and, thinking he was joking, we all laughed.

'It's not funny, I'm serious,' he said. 'I've lost the tickets.' We all went into a panic as we hunted high and low. All the bags were turned out, pockets turned out but still no tickets and only fifteen minutes before check-in. We made our way to the check-in desk to explain our situation and luckily they agreed to issue us with duplicate tickets so all was well again and we were back on course for our holiday in Spain.

We arrived in Alicante at four o'clock in the morning and as we walked to the coach that was to take us to our holiday resort, we couldn't help making comments on how lovely and warm it was, even at that time of the morning. We were driven to our resort by minibus and I remember it was an incredible journey, all through the mountains. There were, we thought, a few hair-raising moments when we thought the driver would go over the edge. Therefore we were glad when we reached our destination. Our accommodation was lovely with a beautiful swimming pool, flower gardens, tennis courts and an apartment that was very large and contained everything we needed for a two-week stay. The children, although they'd had only a short nap on the plane, wanted to explore everything. We did, I recall, take them down to see the beach and I shall always remember it—pure white sand that stretched for at least three miles, and, of course, at that time of the morning it was so still and quite beautiful.

Very early on in the first week we made friends with a Dutch man who ran the local restaurant, or bar, as they are more commonly known in Spain. His friendliness towards us was, we felt, very sincere. He spoilt the children, and Dave and I spent many an hour watching the European Cup on the television in the bar's courtyard whilst having a few cold beers. I remember there were customers of several nationalities and the whole atmosphere was electric.

We spent most of our lazy holiday days swimming, sunbathing and dining out mixed with a little sightseeing. Towards the middle of the second week, the owner of the bar was having a quiet drink with us. We were saying how lovely it was in Spain and how nice it would be to live there, when he, the owner, mentioned that he had a villa for sale, a three-bedroomed villa, with large swimming pool together with two thousand square metres of land. He went on to say that it was situated in the middle of the orange groves. It sounded wonderful, and we all stood there listening to him, mouths agape. He then suggested that he would take us to see it if we would like to and Dave was very quick on the defence, and said, 'Not now, thank you,' to which Wendy and I replied, jumping up and down, 'Oh go on, please. We're only looking.'

Soon Dave was outnumbered and we were all piling into Freek's car to go and see the villa. Although parts of Spain are very wild and uncultivated, everywhere always looked nice in the warm sunshine. The orange trees were all in neat rows, very well cared for and one of the things we liked was that nothing was fenced off. Everything was out in the open and you could walk along the side of the road and pick an orange every few yards if you wished. But to avoid this happening, with so many tourists about, the Spanish would put all the fallen oranges on the top of the culverts that ran alongside the groves, offering them freely, thus preventing damage to their trees. The orange-pickers were always friendly; if you were walking along a long, hot, dusty road they would stop to give you a lift and it didn't matter what they were in—lorry, tractor, donkey or car. I always remember thinking how romantic that was.

We arrived at the villa, and before I could say, 'Behave and be careful,' the children had fled from the car and gone exploring. My first impression was one of beauty. The long gravel path that led up to the house had palm trees lining one side and grapevines on the other. As we reached the house there was an outside staircase that led to a balcony, and below the balcony there was a tiled veranda. The front door was arch-shaped and there was a large arch-shaped window beside it. The gravel path continued at the side of the house and lead to a courtyard with wrought iron gates, also arch-shaped. Behind it was a huge tree covered in bright yellow mimosa in full blossom, providing a large shady area. The view from this courtyard was of an enormous swimming pool, running almost the length of the whole garden and a tiled area surrounding the pool. Beyond the pool was an outbuilding that housed the pumping equipment for the pool and then a flower garden of bright blue flags and fuchsias, growing right up to the back gate, which was also of wrought iron and arch-shaped. Walking down past the opposite side of the house, the gravel path lead to several clothes lines and an outside laundry basin, then on to a double garage at the bottom and, finally, back to the front area, which was the size of two tennis courts, although very overgrown and a little run-down. The whole scene was absolutely beautiful and, just as I was about to fire a hundred questions at Freek, I saw the children running up the stairs to the balcony and within ten seconds of them doing so they were running back down again, screaming.

We all rushed towards them and noticed that they had been

stung several times. 'Hornets,' said Freek. 'I expect you disturbed their nest.' He didn't seem bothered at all and this reassured the children who soon stopped crying and once again ran off to explore. Dave then thought it was time we rounded up the children and got back to the resort and we both thanked Freek for showing us the villa. We all clambered back into his car and returned to our holiday resort where we thanked Freek again and arranged to meet him in his bar that evening as we had done for most of our holiday evenings.

I had been discussing this villa with Dave for most of the rest of the day, being worse than the children, but all the questions I threw at him were beginning to make him feel nervous. 'You could take early retirement,' I said. 'We could sell our house and buy the villa and live in Spain.'

'Think about what you are saying,' Dave said.

'I am,' I replied. 'Don't be an old spoilsport, don't be mean.'

I went on and on, until he finally said, 'I don't want to discuss this any more, all right.'

I agreed, but only until we met Freek that night in the bar because I wanted to know more about the villa, how much he was selling it for, and how easy it was to buy a house in Spain. The children, I remember, were as eager as I was and, looking back now, I realise that I too was still a child in many ways. I remember thinking that the good Lord must have given me gypsy bloody, as I could never settle in one place, always wanting to be on the move. I couldn't sit at home and knit or sew for the children like most mothers and I always seemed to have to be going somewhere or doing something. Dave would always say that he had a job to keep up with me, that he never knew what I was going to do next.

Well, he was soon to find out that evening in the bar. I asked Freek all the questions that I could think of and, when he said that he was selling the villa for seventy-two thousand English pounds, my brain began to tick over. I knew that house prices in the UK had risen sharply in the last year and that we only had a very low mortgage on ours, so I was putting all these figures together in my mind. I remember Wendy saying, 'Are we going to buy that villa and live in Spain?'

So I looked at Dave and Dave looked at me and he said, 'Don't ask me, ask your mother. She's the one who does all these daft things.' We only had a few days left of our holiday and I think I spent every one of them pestering Dave to buy the villa that we had been to see. We spent the last night of our holiday in Freek's bar still talking about the sale of the villa and finally Dave gave way and said we would go back to the UK and give it some serious thought. We said our farewells, and thank-yous for having had such a nice time and left on the coach to Alicante airport. On the flight home that was the topic of conversation—the villa!!

'Oh go on, Dad,' one would say, and then I would say, 'We would be like film stars,' and Dave would say all the sensible things like, 'What about the cost? What about the children's schooling?'

We arrived home tired from travelling with some wonderful memories of a lovely holiday and, of course, a nice suntan. The next day we all were back into our normal routines, school for the children and work for Dave and me. I remember coming home from work that evening and bringing up the subject of buying a villa in Spain whilst I was unpacking from the holiday. I was giving Dave all the reasons why we should and, of course, in turn he would give me all the reasons why we should not. This to-ing and fro-ing went on for most of the evening and, as I had the children on my side, Dave realised he was outnumbered and finally agreed to telephone Freek in Spain and make an offer on the villa. He picked up the telephone and before he dialled the number he looked at me and said, 'I don't believe that I am doing this, Sue. Do you really think that we could sell this house and go and live in Spain?'

'Yes,' I said without even thinking of what I was saying. He then proceeded to dial the number and the children and I sat hovering around the phone. After asking Freek how he was and making general conversation Dave came right out and made him an offer on the villa. There was a further five minutes of conversation and then Dave said, 'Adios mi amigo,' and hung up.

Before he had time to draw breath, I blurted out, 'Well, what did he say?'

Dave said that he had noted our offer and that he needed time to think about it and would ring us in a few days. 'A few days?' I yelled at him. 'That's ages.'

But a few days it was to be. Dave was being very cautious and, as he had said earlier, I went at everything like a bull in a china shop. 'Slow down,' he would always say. 'Think about what you are doing,' but the next few days brought about long discussions, shouting and arguing, and at one stage for several hours we had stopped talking to each other but life went on in between as normal. One week later the telephone rang and it was Freek and after hearing Freek's voice I quickly passed him on to Dave. They had a lengthy conversation and I can remember Wendy and I jumping up and down with our fingers crossed and giggling at each other as if we were going off to the seaside for the day. Of course there was an excuse for Wendy because she was a child and therefore expected to act like one but I was an adult and probably should be acting more seriously.

After the phone call we eagerly asked Dave what Freek had said and he looked at me and said, 'Yes, Freek said he will accept our offer.' Then he went on to explain the terms. He wanted five hundred pounds as a 'good faith' payment and said if we could visit Spain he knew a good solicitor who could sort out the financial side of things. I remember all of us dancing around the room singing, 'We are going to live in Spain,' that was, Wendy, Denis, Dave and I. Sean was now nearly seventeen years of age, was working for a local company, and made it quite clear that he was not going to move to Spain with us. I remember thinking how awful it would be if I had to leave two of my sons behind and as usual, with anything awful that came into my mind, I quickly dismissed it and convinced myself that I could persuade them and everything would be all right.

Dave and I booked a flight and flew to Spain for three days to register with the solicitor and pay over the deposit. I distinctly remember those three days as Dave had a very bad bout of the flu, but because we had already booked and paid, we were fully committed, not having any money to waste.

On the plane we talked of his early retirement, which he had mentioned many times at his work since he married me and was very much convinced that there would not be a problem. He would be just fifty years of age and I would be forty-four and I couldn't help thinking how lucky we would be to retire at such an early age. Of course we had worked out our finances and would come out quite well off with Dave's money for 'long service' and his pension.

Although most of the things I did were very spur of the moment, Dave's planning and plodding came in handy. He worked everything out on paper and was very thorough in thinking things through. Our short trip to Spain turned out to be a mini-nightmare with only a couple of days to get things rolling. Freek introduced us to a solicitor, who was Belgian and spoke seven languages so his English was near perfect. I remember he had papers ready for us to sign, previously organised by Freek, and we paid over the five hundred pounds with the promise of another fourteen thousand-five hundred pounds within six weeks. This was going to put us out on a limb but we were convinced that we could get a bridging loan for a few weeks, and as houses were selling at that time faster than they could get them on the books we felt pretty confident that all would work out well in the long run. Well, I did but I wasn't entirely sure that Dave did. He felt absolutely awful with the flu bug that he had and all he wanted to do was be home in his bed. I kept assuring him that everything would be all right and not to worry, when suddenly I had a flashback to my past: where had I heard those words before?

The whole three days had been a rush from the moment we landed, as we were swept along with the tide, so it was nice to get back home and get Dave feeling well again. Now we had the task of selling the house because everything was going so fast.

The children had told all their friends that they were going to live in Spain. We booked Spanish lessons in the local school evening classes and Dave went to see his boss at work to talk early retirement. I told my employer and gave a month's notice as I needed to be home to make all the necessary arrangements.

The next big step was to convince the bank to lend us fifteen thousand pounds for the next down-payment on the villa. This turned out to be easier than we had expected. We had a good house for collateral and with Dave's lump sum from his job, now assured by his company, which had agreed to him taking early retirement, on the condition that he find someone to replace him who he would train. After we received the money from the bank we made arrangements with Freek to meet him and hand over a banker's draft. Freek was at that time living out the winter months in Holland, so after much discussion we agreed to meet in Belgium. He would drive down from Amsterdam and we would get the ferry over to the port of Zebrugge. Before we knew it, the six weeks had flown by and were on our way to Belgium to hand over the money. We left our car at the docks in Dover, caught the ferry over, met Freek who was on time as we were, handed him the draft and he in turn handed us the papers to sign. I remember neither of us had a pen so we had to borrow one from another passenger.

It was quite an incredible experience—two English people travelling to Belgium to meet a Dutch man to buy a villa in Spain. The whole exercise took just half an hour. We shook hands, said our goodbyes and Freek drove off and we caught the same ferry back on its one-hour turn-around. I remember Dave's face on the return journey; he looked pale, and I tried to convince him that everything would be all right. All he knew was that we had handed over sixteen thousand pounds, had a house to sell in just under three months, children to be responsible for, and a wife whom he must have thought had gone mad. It was done. We were now committed and there was still lots to do. It seemed that I thrived on change—the more there was to do, the more I wanted to do. The house had been up for sale for a few weeks now, and we had had quite a few prospective buyers, but no firm offers. We hired a removal company to pack all our belongings when the time came. We had decided to take everything in the house—all the furniture, all personal effects; everything because we wanted the children to feel at home when they moved. We knew that once the excitement had died down the change would be tremendous for them and we wanted to make it as easy as possible for them, and, of course, ourselves.

In the next few weeks we had some hair-raising experiences with the selling of the house. We had a buyer who had accepted our price, a young couple who were moving to the area with his company. They loved the house and the sale was agreed. We then went ahead and set the date for removal, and booked the ferry for us to sail from Dover to Calais on the 11th July. We would drive down to Denia, making stopovers on the way to enjoy the trip. Everything seemed to be going well, all fitting into place, when we got a call from the estate agents saying the couple buying our house would like to bring their parents around to view. We said they were welcome, fixed a time, and I arranged to be there. When they arrived, I was flabbergasted. The father went over the house like a tornado and he was the rudest man I think I have ever met in my whole life. He then stood outside the front of house and said, 'This house isn't worth what my son is paying for it; you'll be hearing from us again soon.' Without even saying thank-you or goodbye they got in their car and left.

I couldn't believe what had just happened and in desperation I rang Dave at work who advised me to ring the estate agent without delay. They advised us that the prospective buyer had been back in touch with them and had said that they were still interested in buying our house but at five thousand pounds less. I remember asking the estate agents what we should do and they advised that we sit back and call their clients' bluff. We realised we couldn't do this because we were totally committed with the removal, the ferry, all the things that had been paid for and there was no turning back. We needed the money from the house to pay off the remainder on the villa, one thing depending on the other right down the line so we had to drop the price and accept their lower offer.

Very reluctantly that day I rang the agents to accept, and we were back on course again.

All the trauma of trying to get everything to fit into place and at the right time was beginning to tell on our nerves. Dave and I were very jumpy with each other and in all the upheaval I had forgotten that Paul and Sean were not coming with us. I had, if I am honest, accepted that Paul would not be coming; he was making a life for himself, and although we were always in touch with each other he had lived away from home for several years now and was twenty years old. With Sean it was slightly different; he was also making a life for himself but still living at home. He was between seventeen and eighteen and had made it very clear to me that there was definitely no way that he was going to live in Spain. At the time I thought I would be able to persuade him to change his mind. I had been so tied up with all the arrangements, charging off in my usual way like a bull at a gate, that I had taken it for granted that Sean would be coming with us and I did everything in my power to make him change his mind. But he wouldn't budge, and it was after his final decision that I took time out and sat and thought about what I had done.

I started to feel very guilty and thought to myself that in my own eagerness and selfishness I was about to do exactly what I said I would never do. I was going to leave my two sons behind and split up the family. I began to realise that this was the first time that I had really thought about what I was doing, having rushed at everything, pushed and edged Dave on. After all these weeks it had suddenly hit me, but it was too late even to contemplate changing my mind. We had paid all that money, we had sold the house and we had arranged a big leaving party with all our family and friends, but still I kept telling myself that Sean would change his mind and come with us.

We had the farewell party a few days before the packers were due and the two youngest children were very excited and wanted to invite all their school friends, which turned out to be nearly half the school. However, we went along with them as we knew this was going to be a very big step for them. I was still very upset that Sean wasn't coming with us and I was clutching at straws that something, anything, would change his mind. All the family turned up with the exception of Roy and his wife and family, and I loved having everyone together, even my stepfather came assisted by my two sisters and their families. He hadn't enjoyed good health for several years, but still I couldn't bring myself to forgive him and be nice to him. I was, of course, respectful—that was my nature—but each time I saw him I would only be reminded of my past and the sadness that I felt he had brought upon my mother. Roy and his wife not turning up was a disappointment but I had grown used to him being out of my life, and as the years had gone by, the pain seemed to get less and less. I wanted him to be happy but deep down in my heart I knew he, like me, would always be tormented by the past.

It was a nice warm summer evening in July and so many friends as well as family turned up to wish us *bon voyage*, many spilling over into the garden. Dave and I had worked so hard on the garden, to make it look nice, and the fishpond had matured nicely over the last few years, although, every time I looked at the pond, I was reminded of its terrible secret. I have never ever breathed a word to the children, not even to this very day. Bella, our Yorkshire Terrier pet dog, had recently had six puppies. I remember she had been a bit of a scallywag and got out of the garden one day, when she was not supposed to, and the next door neighbours' dog which was probably one of the ugliest dogs in the whole world had 'got' at her. Dave had found them locked together behind the back fence and had had to, with great difficulty, pull them apart, hence the result, nine weeks later, of six puppies. Like all puppies they were adorable and she had given birth to them in the airing cupboard, and every time one was born we would hear Wendy scream with delight and shout, 'That's another,' until there were six.

I recall, at that time, that I was still working; so the puppies along with their mother, Bella, had to be housed in the greenhouse in the garden. I had made it very comfortable for them and each day when I got home from work I would let them out to exercise. On one particular day I had a day off from work and, after the children had gone off to school, I gave the house a good tidy and decided to let the puppies out to play for a while. The front door bell rang and it was a neighbour who had spotted that I was at home and had called round to ask whether I would like to go over to her house for coffee. After chatting at the door for several minutes I invited her in for coffee and to see the puppies. I walked into the garden and all the puppies were running around as usual until I realised that there was one missing. I counted them over and over, and then to my horror I noticed a puppy floating in the fishpond. I hauled it out and tried everything to revive it, but it was too late. I couldn't believe it. I remember hugging it and kissing it and crying and praying for it to come back to life, but it was too late. With the help of my neighbour we put all the puppies back into the greenhouse with Bella, and I buried the dead puppy in the garden. After desperately trying to think how I would tell the children, I decided not to because the puppies were very nearly ready to be sold to good homes. Instead, I set about making a card to advertise them and drove to the nearest shops and put a 'puppies for sale' sign in the shop window. When I got back home I popped round to my neighbours and explained what I had done and asked her to keep the secret with me. Would she please never ever tell anyone that one of the puppies had died? She agreed.

That day the children came home from school at the usual time and as always ran in and said, 'Hello Mum, can we let the puppies out?'

And I replied, 'Yes, but there are only five now because I sold one today,' and amongst the oohs and aahs I watched them roll about playing on the lawn with the puppies. I remember how awful I felt at telling the children a lie, having always insisted whilst bringing them up always to be honest, not to tell lies and here I was, doing just that. They always knew that there was no question of ever keeping any of the puppies—that they were all to be sold and found good homes. It was just the thought of telling them that one had drowned and that it was my fault. I just couldn't bear to tell them and, therefore hurt them, so I never did. I always looked upon the fishpond in a different light from anyone else after that, remembering my hidden secret.

The farewell party was wonderful and my youngest brother's wife had made us a beautiful cake in the shape of a horseshoe for luck, decorated in the Spanish colours of red and yellow; it was lovely. If there was any catering to do for anyone in the family, my sister-in-law would always come up trumps. It was a work of art and tasted as good as it looked.

Everyone seemed to be enjoying themselves when, all too soon, the time came around to say our goodbyes. In a few days we would be off to live in Spain and wouldn't get the chance to see anyone before we left. I remember there were hugs and kisses, tears and promises of 'I will write' and verbally booking dates for their holidays. It was hectic until eventually everyone had gone home with the exception of Paul who was just about to leave with his friends. I remember how sad it was saying goodbye to him, even though he didn't now live with us. I hugged him tightly and I told him how much I loved him and asked him to take care, and selfishly asked him to take all his holidays with us in Spain. We all waved him goodbye and I remember not only feeling sad myself, but wondering how sad the others might be at me breaking up the family. Then, as I had done many times in my life, I stood still and thought about what I was doing. Was it the right thing I asked myself? Did I realise what was ahead of us? Looking back now, I don't think I did. Perhaps I was trying to relive my childhood and somehow anything adventurous seems to excite me.

The party was over, all our goodbyes had been said, except one, and that was Sean. It had been heartbreaking saying goodbye to Paul, but having to leave Sean behind as well was not going to be easy. I had done everything in my power to persuade him to come with us but his mind was made up, he was staying. He had found a bedsit locally and assured me that he would be all right, and that he would keep in touch. I remember as I hugged him tightly and said goodbye how guilty I felt, and for those last few nights I wrestled over and over again with my conscience, telling myself we were committed and that we had to go. Wendy and Denis were so excited; Dave had paid all that money, and we had both left our places of employment, but, deep inside, my heart was breaking. I was breaking up my family and I asked myself why was I such a restless person? Why did I never seem satisfied with the way things were? Why did I always want to change everything?

CHAPTER
FIFTEEN

The big day arrived and everything had gone on to a container with the removal company and would join us in Spain in three weeks. We were going to drive to Denia, and stop and see friends in France on the way. We had packed the car with things for our immediate use, planning to be travelling for approximately one week. We would be able to live for at least two weeks in the villa with the holiday-type of furniture that had been included in the sale by which time our belongings would arrive and hopefully we could settle in to our new surroundings.

Driving to the ferry, we all had mixed feelings. Dave's were of apprehension and fear of the unknown, the children's were of excitement and adventure, and mine I can only describe as being similar to wearing a heavy overcoat—all warm and cosy on the outside but really sad and scared on the inside.

Our journey to Denia was very enjoyable and most interesting. We had prepared the children for a long journey and had furnished them with pens, notebooks, comics, sweets, crisps and all the things that parents bribe children with. They were used to long car journeys as we had always taken lots of weekend trips and Dave would make life interesting with general knowledge questions and quizzes. Because he didn't drive I did all the driving but he would navigate and keep the children from distracting me whilst I was driving.

We caught the evening ferry from Portsmouth to St Malo as we had prearranged an evening stopover at Bordeaux with some work friends of Dave's. They were holidaying in Bordeaux at the time and we had arranged to meet them there and celebrate Bastille Day with them, which we did, and had a wonderful time. They made us feel very welcome and we all went dancing that night in the town and joined in all the celebrations.

We had taken Bella our family pet Yorkshire Terrier with us, and before leaving we had made all the necessary arrangements with the Royal Veterinary Society to get the correct papers for her to travel to Spain with us. I remember it was quite official bringing her into France but nobody seemed interested when we arrived at the Spanish border. There had been no specific paperwork for Spain and we were told that, as long as she had had all her inoculations, there would be no problems. So Bella sat comfortably with Wendy and Denis on the back seat of the car, wondering as we did from time to time, I suspect, what was going on.

After saying goodbye to our newly made friends in Bordeaux we set off once again to continue our journey. Our next stopover was Pamploma and I remember we had all made a loud cheer as we crossed over the border from France into Spain. We soon began to feel the change in temperature; it was getting warmer and warmer and we were all tiring more quickly, and needing to stop more often for refreshments. Pamploma was just somewhere to stop and eat and rest up. Overnight stays in hostels were very easy to obtain in Spain, and we soon found one and got settled in. I do remember on that particular occasion of a funny happening. We had all been shown to our rooms, Denis and Wendy sharing one, Dave and I the other. Dave had noticed that we had no lock on our door, and reported it to the owners, who just shrugged their shoulders and said, 'No pasa nada,' which we understood as meaning 'no problem'. We had been told also that our room was not ensuite, that the bathroom was further down the corridor. We were all keen to freshen up and took turns and Dave, being the perfect gentleman, allowed us to go first. When it was eventually his turn, he seemed to take ages so I went along to see if there was a problem, only to find Dave hiding behind the door clutching a fistful of screws and a lock. He had dismantled the lock from the bathroom door with all the intentions of fitting it on our bedroom door and, as he continued to explain, to put the broken lock that was on our bedroom door back onto the bathroom door. I couldn't believe what I was hearing and relayed the story to the children who by now had joined us. We were soon bent double, bursting our sides with laughter. Still giggling, we decided to hide the disconnected lock behind something in the bathroom, had an enjoyable meal, and retired to our rooms to a good night's sleep with, I might add, no lock on our bedroom door.

We awoke the next morning feeling very refreshed; breakfast was a sort of help-yourself deal—croissants and coffee or coffee and croissants, and already the children were tormenting Dave with their 'Sherlock Holmes' stories.

Bella had also enjoyed a good night's sleep. She was so small we managed to smuggle her into the hostel, and we allowed her to sleep that night with the children. Smuggling the dog into the hostel reminded me that I too was smuggling the children into Spain because when I had received my final divorce papers the judge had ruled, and I quote, 'At no time must the children be taken out of the country without the consent of both the father and the mother until the said children reach the age of seventeen years'. I always knew this but as their father had only ever visited them on two or three occasions at the time of the divorce I took it upon myself to ignore the ruling. I assumed that as I had left the two boys at home he would be assured of my return.

The long journey had been safe and enjoyable and we were now on the last lap. Denia had been signposted as only three kilometres away. We had travelled over sixteen hundred miles and as we drove that last few kilometres all the fun of our two-week holiday came rushing back at us. I don't think that anyone of us, with the exception of Dave maybe, realised that this was going to be permanent. It was like a big fun thing, a long, long holiday in sunny Spain. It all seemed to be wonderful sun, sea and sand, where nothing could go wrong, or would it?

Tired, hot and very weary from travelling, we arrived at the villa that was to be our new home. Dave and I were very happy that we had arrived safely, the children were just happy that we had arrived. They soon dashed off to explore. Freek had left a message earlier with us telling us where he would leave the key and sure enough there it was. We also noticed how he had left everything tidy for us. The villa was sparsely furnished—not with anything fabulous—but there was enough to be going on with until our furniture arrived.

The children had already chosen their bedrooms. Wendy, sixteen now, had chosen the large bedroom which was ensuite and had its own front door leading out on to the red-tiled veranda. Denis had drawn the shorter straw of the two and had the middle bedroom, sharing Wendy's bathroom. Denis was twelve years old and at that age he didn't seem to care if he even had a bedroom. Wendy and Denis were very close as brother and sister and this adventure only enhanced that closeness. There was one other bedroom that led into the lounge and it already had been agreed by Dave and I that this would be ours.

The kitchen was fitted with pale blue units; the lounge had a black and white tiled floor with a wood-burning stove, and a lovely arch-shaped window. Another bathroom led from the kitchen which I immediately thought would be illegal in England because of only having one door between kitchen and loo. Leading from the other side of the lounge was a beautiful conservatory. This was to be my favourite room and it had been, we suspected, built on at a later date. It had large windows all the way round and a bright, light-tan tiled floor. It also had double sliding patio doors leading into the courtyard where the huge mimosa tree stood in the middle giving lots of shade. The yellow blossom that we had seen the previous time on this tree was just about to reappear and, of course, through two black arch-shaped wrought iron gates was the huge swimming pool which was the main attraction of the villa. Freek had cleaned it and filled it with fresh water and it was a bluey-green colour shimmering in the sunlight.

Before we had time to start unpacking the car, the children had pleaded with us to go for a swim. I remember saying to them that there was no hurry for anything, having promised them that they could have one month before we thought about settling them into the environment. Dave and I needed to do the same. So 'Yes,' I said, 'we can all go for a swim.' After the first few anxious minutes we were splashing about as if we had been doing this all our lives. Dave didn't swim and had quite a fear of water. In fact we had often made jokes about living in Spain with a swimming pool when he couldn't swim. I remember that very first time in the swimming pool, listening to the children laughing and splashing about, seeing how happy they were and for a brief moment thinking how wonderful it would have been if the two boys had been with us too. I had been in touch with them several times by telephone whilst we were travelling and to say that we had arrived safely. Although the public telephone system was expensive in Spain there were always plenty of phones available. I had made a promise to the boys that I would write to them both every week. This, I felt, would make them feel like I hadn't abandoned them.

The first four weeks were wonderful, and we soon made good friends with our new neighbours. They were a Dutch couple with a young baby. Their house was not too close to ours, there being a large empty field between us, which was used sometimes by the locals to put their horses. Our neighbours on the other side of us were also Dutch and, although much older, they were friendly, but kept themselves to themselves. If there was anything we were not sure of we would ask our young neighbours, Ted and Annette. Annette was able to speak seven languages and offered to help Denis and Wendy with their learning of Spanish. Those first few weeks we had much to talk about, and I remember Annette asking if Wendy would like to help her out for a few hours a week with the baby and some light housework. Wendy was very grateful as it would give her some spending money. There was lots of oohs and aahs from Denis but we explained that he would be going to school soon and would need all his spare time studying. I can see that Dave and I used Ted and Annette for most of our language translations in those early days. They had been in Spain for several years and knew all the ropes, so to speak, and as their knowledge of English was very good we found them extremely helpful. They too were very kind to the children and helped out whenever they could.

After spending every day swimming and lazing in the sunshine and cleaning the villa to suit our needs and pottering in the gardens which were very overgrown and would need lots of tender loving care, the next item on our agenda was to be the arrival of our furniture.

Although Dave and I enjoyed the first few weeks with the children lazing and sunbathing there was so much for us to learn. We could only speak very little Spanish and after having a real close inspection of the villa, as one only does after the purchase, we began to find several problems. We had discovered that there were problems with the electrics. Denis on one occasion was adjusting a picture on his bedroom wall when he received quite a nasty electric shock and Dave found out later that there wasn't any earth wiring anywhere. We also discovered that the cooker was attached to a gas cylinder bottle and that we had to go to a gas depot to replace the empty ones with full ones. We could only exchange one for one, we could not purchase another without going to an office in town and filing out mounds of forms only to be told that the previous owner was responsible for leaving four gas bottles not two.

Dave and I knew that Freek had his bar up for sale and that he himself had gone back to Holland to live. We did hear rumours that one could buy a spare gas bottle for twenty-five pounds on the open market, empty ones of course, and that it was a fineable offence if one got caught. We had also been told by the authorities that we should have a gas contract and that we would have to pay fifty pounds for this, which we did. I remember taking this contract to the gas depot and being told, 'Sorry, no empty, no fill,' and, believe it or not, we never came across the opportunity to get spare gas bottles from anywhere. We managed for three years with just the two. It just meant that we made twice as many trips to the depot.

We soon began to realise after some of the trips what we were up against. We were approached by the locals—the land-owners of the surrounding orange groves—who said that they were collecting money from all the surrounding properties who used the dirt-track access road, to pay for a new road. They were going to tarmac it. I remember paying over five hundred pounds for this and after waiting what seemed to be a lifetime for this new road, eventually the workers turned up with their machine and set about laying the thinnest layer of tarmac one ever saw. There was no edging to the job, hence, with the hot sun burning down for most of the days, the tarmac started to melt and crumble away, leaving great big holes. Then, when the rains came, these holes would fill up and the holes would get bigger and bigger. We often made jokes about there being a little bit of road in between the holes.

Another learning exercise we encountered was after our neighbours had informed us to order some logs for the winter. They explained to us that these houses were lovely in summer, as they were built to keep cool; therefore in winter they were also very cold and could feel very damp. So we set about ordering in our best Spanish language a delivery of logs for our wood-burning stove and to our amazement the very next day this lorry turned into our drive and tipped out the biggest load of logs I have ever seen. We immediately thought that we had made a mistake with our figures in the translation, but as it was too difficult to explain we paid, tipped the driver, thanked him and waved him goodbye.

With the help of the children, the logs were all stacked against the side of the house, and it turned out that when the winter months came that 'load of logs' only lasted a few weeks, which soon made us realise that this was going to be another very costly exercise.

Then there was the private health insurance to sort out. We had heard some horrific stories of people with no insurance being left on the side of the road after an accident. Feeling it was a major priority, especially having two children with us, we set off into town to sort out the insurance. It turned out to be quite straightforward to arrange with an English company but the fee was very expensive, well in excess of two thousand pounds for the four of us. I remember Dave and I looking at each other and pulling a face but we knew it had to be paid and we paid it.

That day, whilst we were in town, we decided to look at the English private schools and although Wendy had finished school and passed her exams in the UK we felt that a couple of years in college learning Spanish would be good for her. Unfortunately, we immediately had to rule out private education as the quarterly fees were astronomical. I remember being quoted over eight hundred pounds per child per term, which would have left us broke after a couple of years. We then explained to the children that they would have to go to Spanish state schools, and I remember that it didn't seem to bother Denis but Wendy pulled a few faces.

We had promised the children that they could wait just a few more weeks before signing them in for school, at least until the furniture arrived, and then they should feel more settled and more at ease with going to a strange school.

It had been over five weeks now and still no furniture lorry. We had used Annette's telephone so many times to ring the company involved, it was becoming an embarrassment. We were all getting very edgy but we rang again and were told that there had been a small hiccup and that delivery time was going to be longer than expected. 'How much longer?' we asked. Finally, after spending over sixty-five pounds on telephone calls and speaking to three different managers in the company, and eighteen weeks from our date of arrival we were told that the removal lorry would be with us that day. Eighteen weeks—we could not believe that we had waited so long and we were very quick to remember how much this removal had cost us and Dave said he would be writing to their head office for compensation.

We all, I am sure, remember that day like no other. The lorry arrived, and as it turned into the driveway, taking half the wall with it, we cheered and drank champagne.

We were soon to realise that there were a few other hiccups along with the arrival of our belongings. First, the driver was all alone so Dave and I had to help unload, and the numerous trips up and down the driveway were, to say the least, exhausting. Secondly, there were several items broken, which we found hard to understand as we had been told at the onset that once everything was on the container it would stay untouched until it arrived in Spain. But this, as we were unloading, soon proved otherwise. Thirdly, there were several things missing—nothing major—and of course as we found out later, they were never to be seen again.

Despite taking all these things into account, we were still so pleased to have our belongings. The children were going crazy tearing open boxes and yelling, 'This is mine, oh look,' and they spent the rest of that day, and several days to follow, laying out all their things neatly in their rooms. Dave and I were also excited and I remember throwing ourselves onto our sofa and chairs and sighing with the comfort of them. There was also the joy of having all our kitchen appliances, and our own bed and wardrobes; the whole list was endless. We really did appreciate that day, and thought that absence really does make the heart grow fonder.

After what seemed to be complete chaos in our lives we had now been in Spain for nearly six months and now had some kind of a routine. The children had been settled into their schools, Wendy having registered with a Spanish college. She was sixteen and it was a very difficult age to be plunged into an all-Spanish-speaking class.

I remember her first day couldn't have been worse for her. Our car had broken down and our neighbours Ted and Annette very kindly offered me the use of their car until we could get it repaired. I set off early in the morning with Wendy and managed to get halfway to the college when the car came to a halt with a flat tyre. I remember we both got out of the car and just stood in the road, which was in the middle of nowhere, and looked at each other in disbelief. 'Come on,' I said, 'we'll change the wheel.' I had watched several people over the years change tyres and had a very good idea how it was done. We hunted everywhere on that car for a spare wheel and couldn't find one.

Wendy was near to tears now. She had explained to me that it was already embarrassing going into a classroom that didn't speak her language, let alone going in late. I then suggested that she would have to walk and that I would walk far enough with her to find a telephone. No sooner had I said this than it started to rain. It hardly ever rains in Spain but at this precise time, when Wendy was so upset about being late for school, it did. I knew how she felt; it wasn't the actual rain that mattered; it just seemed that it was the last straw when everything was going wrong. I could see myself in her so much at times like this, and all I wanted to do was to take away the hurt from her. I knew it was really only a minor incident in her life so whilst we walked along the road together I explained this to her and, as more often than not, we looked at each other, smiled and later laughed about the whole situation.

The story of the flat tyre however turned out to be a nightmare. I managed to ring Ted who informed me on the phone that there was no spare wheel and went on to say that if I purchased one he would reimburse me. Having been such nice neighbours for lending me the car in the first place, I readily agreed. I went to the garage and the owner took me back to the car and fitted a new tyre. I paid him and returned home with a receipt for fifty-two pounds, which, on my return, I gave to Annette. After a period of nearly six weeks Dave and I were casually discussing the incident with the flat tyre and reminded ourselves that we had never been paid the fifty-two pounds by Ted or Annette. As Dave had invited Ted around for a drink that evening he said he would mention it to him, in a nice sort of way so as not to offend, which is what he did. To our amazement, Ted said that he had given the money to his wife, Annette, to give to us that same day. Imagine how embarrassed we were! It wasn't long before we were able to put the pieces together and realise that it was on that same day that Annette went out and bought a new puppy, and that we understand that there had been a massive argument because of this. As it turned out, Ted paid us the money but, sadly, our friendship with our Dutch neighbours was never quite the same again.

Denis' first day at school was also a day to remember. He was twelve years old and the school that we had registered him with was almost three miles form the villa. Therefore I would be driving him to school each day and collecting him. On the first day he, like Wendy, had been very nervous and although he had more of an easy-going nature the thought of the unknown was obviously quite scary to a youngster. I remember driving him in the car and telling him, 'Don't worry, everything will be all right,' and once again I day-dreamed for a few seconds, remembering Roy and me all those years ago.

We arrived at the school just outside the town centre to find hundreds of children in the playground. They were all awaiting their names to be called and allocated their classrooms for the new term. I remember every single word was in Spanish and Denis waited almost three hours to hear his name called until eventually we were the only ones left in the playground. Then a male teacher looked in our direction and beckoned Denis to come forward. I remember Denis holding my hand tightly and looking at me with spaniel eyes, saying, 'Please don't leave me, Mum.'

At that moment I felt that I wanted to hug and hold him so tightly and never ever let him go. The teacher came towards him wearing a warm and caring smile and explained in very broken English that he would take care of my son and for me not to worry. It had been explained to me at the registration through an interpreter that Denis would be placed into a classroom with all Spanish-speaking children and that he would learn very quickly. It was also pointed out, in a very polite and friendly way, that the teachers had very little individual time to give to foreign children but that they were very welcome to join their schools.

I left the school that day with tears in my eyes watching Denis look back at me as the teacher led him into the building. So I promised myself that if he was going to be one bit unhappy and didn't like it in a foreign school, then I would take them back to England. I never told Dave at that time of my promise but I knew in my heart that I meant it.

Making all sorts of excuses to get to the school early that afternoon, I sat patiently waiting in the car for Denis. I heard the school bell and immediately stepped from the car only to find after a few seconds crowds of children all trying to clamber through the gates at the same time. I remember standing on tiptoe to see if I could catch a glimpse of Denis and at the same time feeling a little nervous of being swept round and round by all the children rushing past me, and talking a language that I couldn't understand. Then I saw Denis coming towards me with two or three other boys of a similar age and as he reached me he introduced me to them as '*mi madre*' (my mother). How a person can go from sadness to such happiness in one moment? I cannot explain except that I did. From that day onwards Denis mixed with Spanish children and learnt their language and went on to pass his exam in fluent Spanish.

Wendy was still finding it a little difficult to mix with Spanish girls of her own age at college because they, of course, had a head start on her with the language. At sixteen, as I could well remember, it is a very difficult age to start something new. She left after a few months and took up some part-time jobs with the neighbours to enable her to earn some spending money but being so close to her young brother, Denis, she soon went on to master the Spanish language. I remember in my letters to the boys that I would say how proud I was of Wendy and Denis, yet always being careful never to upset them by praising one child more that the other.

CHAPTER SIXTEEN

For a long time afterwards, life just sailed by and we were all enjoying ourselves. Dave and I passed away the time busying ourselves in the garden and, for Wendy and Denis, after their school hours it was friends, swimming, sunshine and laughter. Dave and I had many social gatherings with friends and an odd meal or game of cards with the neighbours. There was one special bar we would frequent on Sunday lunchtimes in the main town. A group of English musicians would get together each week and entertain us by playing jazz and that's where we met two very lovely people who went on to become our very best friends—Bill and Leila.

Bill came over to our table said that he thought he recognised Dave from somewhere and after a lengthy elimination process and a few more beers they both agreed that they had met sometime during their air force careers. We were then invited to join them at their table and they went on to tell us their story of how they had come to live in Spain. They were from Liverpool and had four married daughters. Bill had retired from the air force after almost thirty-two years and Leila was a head nurse. They told us how they had set up their own nursing home in the UK and how hard they had worked for several years before selling up, during the property boom, much the same as us, and retiring to Spain. I remember it was friendship at first sight and we had so much in common. We were both very close to our families, were Catholics, smoked cigarettes like they were going out of fashion as they were so cheap in Spain, and we all liked a drink, although I didn't really indulge very much. I would have a glass of wine now and then to be sociable but I wasn't a drinker in those earlier days. I was more of an eater and that was one thing that Leila and I didn't have in common. Leila could entertain and she could make a three-course meal out of goodness-knows-what and always a dessert for me. Whatever the time of day she would lay the table with best china, serviettes, candles, wine and would always make everyone feel welcome. They took to Wendy and Denis like their own and there was nothing that they wouldn't do for us and right up to this very day they hold a very special place in our hearts.

We had now reached the stage when we had had a telephone installed. The waiting list when we applied was miles long but with a few tips from our neighbours and a good few extra pesetas we won the day. It was heaven sent for me because I could now telephone the boys as often as we could possibly afford and sometimes more often when Dave wasn't around.

I had taken up letter-writing with a passion and I wrote to everyone—my two sisters, my youngest brother, and all my friends. I kept my promise and wrote separate letters to Paul and Sean every single week. I still had no contact with Roy although I had heard that he was busy getting on with his life much the same as I was. I did write to Alan in Canada more often now and I still kept in contact with my Irish friends in Dublin at the motor company at least once a year and would remember some of the good times I had enjoyed living in Dublin. I would always remember dearest Sean and Flo and Ma. They too all held a special place in my heart.

I was also still corresponding with my two doctor friends in Australia and would often get a nice letter and a couple of photos from them, triggering my memory to go back all those years, thirty-three, to be exact. Although some memories had faded, others were still very much with me. Sadly, it's mostly the good memories that fade and the nightmare ones that remain. But I always loved letter-writing, I always felt this need to keep in touch and, no matter how brief the memory in my life was, I felt I must hang on to it.

Most of my letter-writing paid off because when I wrote to people I always invited them to come and visit us in Spain and we had so many visitors we decided to keep a visitors' book. It was always wonderful to see everybody, especially the two boys and their friends. When they arrived, I would sit by the side of the pool, watching them swimming with Wendy and Denis. I would look at all four of them and tears of joy would fill my eyes as I thought over and over how lucky I was, and how much I loved them, and that, if the world caved in, my arms would be plenty big enough to go all around them and lift them to safety.

We had been living in Spain now for almost two years and, like most days, we were busying ourselves when the telephone rang. Dave answered it, thinking it was one of the boys and worrying what it would cost them. I dashed to the phone. I heard Dave saying, 'Just a moment and I will ask her. If you give me your number, I will get her to call you back.' He scribbled down a telephone number and put the phone down.

'Who was that?' I asked him.

I remember he looked quite pale and said to me, 'You had better sit down.'

I felt as though my stomach had disappeared into my throat, and I was now yelling, 'Who was it?' He said it was a man asking if I had given birth to a baby daughter on a certain day in 1960. He had said that he was the husband of this 'daughter' who was now thirty-one years of age and that she had been trying to trace her real mother and had traced her to me. I think I just sat there and glared at Dave for what seemed like a whole week. My legs were shaking, my stomach was still in my throat and I felt numb. Dave made me a cup of tea whilst I got my thoughts together and I remember getting up and going straight to a drawer where we kept our paperwork and sifting through the papers. I knew exactly where the birth certificate was and walking towards Dave, waving it in my hand, I knew that it was my daughter 'Heidi' who had found me.

After I managed to compose myself, I nervously dialled the telephone number that Dave had jotted down. A voice said, 'Hello,' and after a long pause a conversation took place. This 'lady' was my daughter Heidi who had been taken from me all those years ago and adopted. She explained to me on the telephone that her adopted parents had been wonderful to her; they had changed her name to Kathy and she had had a good life but always wanted to know who her real mother was and why she had given her away. I could not believe that I was having this conversation. How incredible that after thirty-two years it should stir up so many memories, both good and bad. She went on to tell me that she was married and had two children, a girl and a boy. At the end of our conversation I promised her I would send her a letter explaining all that happened all those years ago and suggested that perhaps she would do the same for me and tell me all about her life. I put the telephone down and sat down in awesome wonder to give myself time to take it all in. Dave had known my secret and when Wendy was nearly fourteen years old I had told her in the hope that she would not make the same mistakes as I had but I had never told the boys, never really having had any reason to until now.

That night I put pen to paper and wrote dozens of pages to Kathy, giving her all the information, and more, that she asked for. I asked for photographs and I enclosed photographs and I felt so excited, but kept questioning myself. Was I excited? How would I deal with this? Wendy had always been my only daughter after Denise had died and now I might have to share her. Could I do that? And would I know this thirty-year-old lady? I could only remember a six-week-old baby. I posted the letter the next day, and I also took time to sit and write to the two boys and explain that they had a half sister. I remember apologising for not telling them. I could have told them by telephone but I thought this was more personal. I had also told Wendy and Denis about the telephone call and they were so pleased for me I just could not believe their response. Although I was so very happy with the news, I was still very unsure how I was going to deal with it. My uncertainty was answered two weeks later when I got a letter from Kathy with photographs. I tore open the letter and immediately looked at the photos and there right in front of my eyes was my baby daughter all grown up—it was like looking at myself and Wendy. Tears filled my eyes and memories came flooding back. Only I could see her 'Elvis look-alike' father in her and although I had no feelings for him all the sadness of those times returned. I read her letter and she said that now she had found me and I had told her the circumstances she could understand. She was so pleased to have brothers and sisters and asked if it would be possible for us to meet. Ironically, she lived only eighty miles from where we used to live in the UK.

We did meet. We planned a special trip from Spain to the UK and went to visit Kathy and her family and my sister allowed us the use of her home to have a family get-together. All the children and a few friends were there to meet Kathy and her family. The children were wonderful, the boys' acceptance was overwhelming, and for me another piece of the puzzle of life was put in place.

Soon after our meeting, Kathy and her family moved to Scotland but we continued to correspond and on my birthday I always get a card which reads, 'Happy Birthday to my dearest mother.'

Very shortly after all this excitement, my concentration was on Wendy. She was a very attractive young lady now and had made several Spanish friends but was still uncomfortable with the language. She had many Spanish boys chasing after her and like all teenagers she was of course flattered. I imagine she loved every minute of it, but our concerns, went much deeper than that. The Spanish people are of a very different culture with a different outlook on life and one thing they regale in is staying out all night, partying, discoing or just entertaining. This is mostly the result of a warm climate so when Wendy first asked us if she could go to the local disco and her dad said, 'Yes, but be home by eleven o'clock,' she simply replied, 'Oh Mum, tell him they don't start till midnight.'

After much discussion we allowed her to go as we felt that we had brought the children here, so therefore we must allow them to live like the Spanish people. Yet we found it very hard to come to terms with Wendy coming up the drive at seven-thirty in the morning and tried our best to accept it as Wendy had always been a very open child. They all had—so we trusted her. Then one day out of the blue she came home from town and said, 'Guess what, Mum? I have met this English girl,' going on to say that they were of similar age and how wonderful it was that this new-found friend could speak English. I was happy for her but then a few days later, things started to go a little too fast. Wendy and her friend were in the house when Wendy said, 'Mum, can I go and live with Maria in her flat in town?' And I, being very used to having a teenage daughter, very calmly responded by saying, 'Yes, Wendy, when you have a full-time job and enough money to pay your share of the rent.'

There was an immediate slam of the eyelids, a walk-out, slamming door and a string of mumbling words of which I heard the tail-end: 'Well I'm going to, anyway.'

I left things as they were and decided to wait until Wendy came home later that day and I could ask her to tell me a few things about her friend. It turned out that her friends' parents were in the UK and apparently paying for her flat in Spain and that she was quite a bit older than Wendy and very, what I would call, worldly wise. I didn't want to interfere too much and spoil Wendy's new friendship as I knew that speaking English was very important to Wendy so I left things alone for a while, although only for a short while.

They had gone out together one evening and Wendy asked what time she should be home and we said, 'Twelve o'clock,' and we got the usual: 'Oh Mum, please Dad.' But we remained firm, and explained that it was a week night and that she was working at the neighbours the following morning, therefore we felt that twelve o'clock was a reasonable time. Off she went in a semi-sulk as teenagers do. Then at approximately eleven forty-five that evening, the telephone rang and it was Wendy asking in an innocent voice what time she had to be home. Trying to stay calm, knowing that this was a typical teenage ploy (after being one myself), I answered by saying, 'Twelve o'clock, Wendy.' Then I got the pleading. 'Twelve o'clock, Wendy,' I repeated.

Then I heard a voice, a voice I knew to be her friend's, say, 'Just say no, Wendy, just say you're not coming home at all, you can stay here.'

Then Wendy said, 'No, Mum, I'm not coming home, I'm going to stay here.'

I was very shocked but tried to stay calm and then I was doing the pleading. 'Please, Wendy, come home and we can discuss it in the morning.'

Then I heard her friend say, 'Just put the phone down,' and with that the line went dead. This was the very first time that Wendy had really defied me. I became angry and at the same time very worried, not even knowing where she was. Leaving a note for Denis in case he woke, Dave and I got in the car and drove off to try and find her. We knew most of the teenage 'hangouts' but everywhere we went Wendy wasn't there. After driving round for what seemed forever, we went home realising it was a hopeless situation—like looking for a needle in a haystack—and also worrying about leaving Denis alone for too long. I didn't sleep a wink that night, making cups of tea, walking up and down. Why was she doing this I would ask myself? I knew why: she was growing up, she had met an English-speaking girlfriend and was afraid of losing her and would do anything to keep her friendship. I knew all this; I knew this wasn't deliberate defiance, but it worried me, the more so I think because of being in a foreign country.

Morning came early for me and my next step came out of sheer panic. I rang Paul and explained the whole situation and how worried I was and he responded straightaway by saying, 'Send her back home here, Mum, I will look after her.' He was sharing a flat with his girlfriend and, although it was only a one-bedroomed flat, he said that Wendy could use the sofa and stay as long as she liked or maybe until she was able to get a job and be able to sort things out for herself. So, being a Sagittarius and always doing everything in haste, I agreed with Paul and thanked him for offering to help his sister and said I would get her on a plane that day and would ring him with the flight times. That's what I did. I booked her a one-way flight to the UK for early that evening from Valencia.

Wendy came home at ten-thirty that morning. She came into the villa very sheepishly and very, very sorry. In fact, we both ended up apologising to each other. We were not only mother and daughter, we were also best friends. I knew she was truly sorry for what she had done and I didn't want to harp on about it too much. I made us both a cool drink and asked her to sit at the table with me as I had something important to tell her. I had gone over and over the words in my own mind before she came home, making sure to get them right. I was in fact taking away her life and changing it to what I thought would be best for her so I had to try and make her understand that I thought my decision would be the right one. Sitting there, telling her all this, made me feel so guilty but it was because I cared about her so much. I tried to explain to her that I didn't want her to go 'downhill' in life. I wanted everything that was wonderful for her. I told her that I had booked her on a flight back to the UK that evening and how much I loved her and hopefully later on in her life she would understand my reasons for doing this. I will never forget the look of shock and surprise on her face but I also sensed that there was a glimmer of excitement because, although she loved Spain with its warm sunny climate and free way of living, somehow she would be glad to be back with her friends and her own culture. She felt that's where she belonged and really wanted to be although the present circumstances of her return were not ideal. Sometimes the quick way is the best way, I thought. I knew that I would be broken-hearted when she left and in my haste I had not taken into account how Denis would feel. They were so close that I soon realised that by parting them there was a real danger of Denis going 'downhill' too.

We drove her to the airport that evening and I thought I would die when I waved this now beautiful young lady off into the big wide world on her own. I knew she needed some guidance and that Paul and Sean would be there for her but looking at her I also knew that she was more than capable and that the relationship we had together would always be special even though there would be a few ups and downs. The foundations had been laid and I felt we would always be there for each other.

During the next few months the boys and Wendy came and spent their holidays with us. Denis had missed Wendy so much and every time I saw them altogether I wept tears of joy but they were growing up and, although it was so hard for me, I had to let them go. I remember Denis asking if he could go and stay with them for the coming Christmas. Dave and I agreed that we would all go, then, after last-minute changes, we decided to stay in a hotel in Benidorm with Bill and Leila for a few days to celebrate the festive season. To avoid Denis being disappointed, I asked if my sister could have Denis for two weeks over the Christmas period because she had a son who was the same age as Denis and when they were younger they more or less grew up together. Finally, it was all agreed that we would spend Christmas in Benidorm with our friends and Denis would travel to the UK, by plane, and stay with my youngest sister and her family. They lived very near to Paul and Sean, and now Wendy, so it would be convenient for everyone.

We took Denis to the airport and waved him goodbye. I had packed his case with Christmas presents for everyone back home and also a present for Denis with strict instructions not to open it before Christmas day. There is a special service at most airports that look after children travelling on their own and we had arranged for this service for Denis.

During that two weeks we had kept in touch with all the children by telephone and my sister, and had reports back that a good time was being had by everyone.

The day arrived when Denis was due back; we had arranged with the Spanish airport authorities to put him on to the coach to Denia, and we would meet him. That morning, Dave and I had early-morning coffee in town and then at ten-thirty we made our way to meet Denis from the coach. The coach arrived on time and we watched the passengers alighting one by one. I remember being all excited, waiting for Denis and we continued waiting until the very last passenger got off. I remember becoming quite agitated and I asked some of the passengers if they had seen a fifteen-year-old boy. With that one of the passengers answered me and said, 'Oh, it must be your boy then,' and went on to say that their flight had been delayed due to a passenger not turning up. Apparently there had been a real mix-up as this missing passenger had checked in with luggage, and had then gone missing.

I felt myself turn to jelly and all sorts of pictures came into mind. Where was he? If he had checked in what had happened to him? I thought perhaps he had gone to the toilets and that someone had molested him; I thought of all sorts of horrid things. I turned to Dave and yelled, 'Do something, please do something.' We ran to the booking agent at the top of the main street and asked them to find my son. I will always remember Dave explaining the situation to them and the agent, who was English, replied, 'Oh well, there's always one idiot.'

With that, Dave grabbed this man by the collar of his jacket and said, 'Where is my son? You find him now.' I had never, in all the years I had known Dave, ever seen him aggressive or raise his voice to anyone.

The agent then responded very quickly, asked us to calm down and said he would telephone Gatwick Airport and find out what had happened. He said that it would be better if we went home and sat by the telephone as Denis, or a member of the family, might be trying to contact us and that he would ring us the minute he had any information. At the time I was very reluctant to do this but eventually saw the sense in it.

The minute I got home I rang my sister asking her whether she knew where Denis was and at the same time I said that he was missing. She then told me that she hadn't been able to take him to the airport; therefore she had put him on the midnight bus the previous night, so he would have been there on time for his early morning flight. I remember I was really angry with her on the phone, calling her irresponsible and all sorts of other awful names; then I hung up.

I decided that I just couldn't sit there in the hope that the phone might ring; I would ring Paul and Sean to see if they knew anything. Just as I was about to dial their number, the phone rang. It was the travel agent to say that they had located my son. I was so relieved. Apparently, Denis had arrived at Gatwick from the all-night coach, had checked in his luggage and, being so tired from his night's travel, had fallen asleep in the departure lounge. When the tannoy calls went out for passengers to board, he had not heard any of them, and nobody could remember checking him in as there had been a staff changeover. Therefore his luggage, which had been checked in, had gone onto the plane but there was no passenger to accompany it. Airport rules are of course, no passenger, no luggage. Once they had removed his luggage, they were then concerned that it bore an Irish surname hence they put his luggage, consisting of one suitcase with skateboard attached, in the middle of the runway to 'blow it up'. Then, this fifteen-year-old woke up two hours later, realised he had missed his plane, began to get frightened and went to the phone to call his brother, Paul. Only having one pound in money left over as he had spent all his money on food on the coach trip in an attempt to stay awake, he dialled the number. Paul answered but was asleep in bed and dropped the phone. Denis could hear him snoring. 'Paul, Paul,' he continued to shout until his money ran out. Then, with tears in his eyes, he went to the check-in desk where, after a few minutes, they realised that Denis was the missing passenger who had caused all the commotion. They then arranged for him to travel on the next available flight to Alicante and also managed to save his luggage from destruction.

All's well that ended well. Denis arrived much later but safely in the care of a mature couple who had had strict instructions from the airline not to let Denis out of their sight, explaining that we, his parents, would be at Alicante to meet him.

Denis arrived, smiling all over his face, and we thanked his appointed guardians sincerely. After I had stopped hugging Denis to the point where I nearly crushed all his ribs, we made our way home. There had been one small hiccup: Denis' luggage was missing but we were informed at the airport that when it was located they would deliver it to our door. We found this hard to believe with all that had gone on but were so pleased to have Denis back safely that his luggage didn't seem very important just then. I remember on the way home we were discussing this and Denis had already decided that he would be putting in an insurance claim for three Rolex watches, two pairs of the most expensive trainer shoes and everything else imaginable that a fifteen-year-old boy might want to possess.

We spent most of that evening listening to Denis' adventure, when, around nine-thirty, there was a loud knock on the window. Bearing in mind that the villa was very isolated, over forty miles from the airport and approximately three miles deep into the orange groves, it was with some surprise that we opened the door to an airport official holding Denis' suitcase and skateboard. As Dave and I and Denis looked at each other and smiled, we had to agree that this time the English had got it wrong and the Spanish had got it right.

All these events led us to think more and more about Denis' future. He wasn't learning very much academically at the Spanish school as he had been so occupied with learning the language. His attitude had also changed considerably after Wendy had left and after his two-week holiday at Christmas he had said how much he had loved it and how well he had got on with his two brothers and sister. Like Wendy, although he loved so much about Spain, he missed his roots, so we talked at length about him going back and staying with Paul and Sean. But I knew already that they had both done more than their fair share towards persuading him.

As it turned out Paul, Sean and Wendy decided to come and

stay with us for a week's holiday. Denis loved this, but no one loved it more than me and I can still see them all walking up the path together, arms linked, laughing and joking. I always felt like I wanted the clocks to stop all over the world at times like this so we could be held in a timelock forever, but I knew real life wasn't like that and simply enjoyed every precious minute.

When it was time for them to return home, Denis asked us if he could go back with them. Although I didn't want to lose him, I wasn't surprised at his request. Once again I felt my eyes fill with tears and I knew this was my last child about to leave home and he was only fifteen. I felt ridden with guilt but realised that the circumstances that I had created had caused this. Seeing the look of longing on Denis' face, I said, 'Yes,' but made it very clear that he was to stay with my other sister and attend school and that Dave and I would, as soon as possible, travel over and settle everything with her. My eldest sister had always said that if Denis wanted to stay with her she would be delighted to have him, so I rang her and made all the arrangements.

We drove them all back to Alicante Airport in the hope that we would be able to buy Denis a ticket at the airport as I did not want him to travel alone again. I remember we were late arriving and the other three had to go straight through to board whilst we tried to sort out a single ticket for Denis. The officials had agreed a price of sixty pounds and Dave offered to pay by credit card but we were promptly told this was not possible—it was a cash deal only. We rushed to the nearest cash-point dispenser only to find that after two attempts we were refused cash. 'Try again,' I said. 'Third time lucky.'

Dave always laughed at all my superstitions and gave a little chuckle when the cash came out on the third time. The hostess took the money and said to Denis, 'You will have to be quick.' I remember hugging Denis and telling him to be good, and to keep in touch, and that Dave and I would be over very soon. We hugged and kissed again and running after the hostess he looked back and shouted, 'Thanks, Mum and thanks, Dad. I love you,' and he was gone, out of sight.

Denis had wanted to stay with his real father for a while, 'only to see what he's like' he had said, and, because his father lived in the same surrounding area, Paul had arranged it. I felt strongly that I couldn't deny Denis the same chance that the others had had during their teenage years. I left strict instructions with Denis that if at any time he was unhappy he was to go straight to my sister's and then she would telephone me. It was only two days after Denis had gone there that I had a phone call from my sister saying that Denis was safe and sound with her and for me not to worry. I remember I promised her on the telephone that we would be over as soon as possible to settle Denis into a new school and make a payment to her for his keep.

Within a week of Denis leaving, we booked a flight to the UK stayed with my sister for a few days and settled Denis into his new school. We knew that it would be very difficult for him to go back to an English school, being so far behind academically, but long-term we both felt very strongly that this was the right road for Denis to take.

CHAPTER SEVENTEEN

We had decided to sell the villa soon after Wendy had gone back to the UK. We had lived in Spain at that time for almost three years and there were of course good times and bad times. Dave and I had enjoyed some wonderful times and so had the children but there were nearly always obstacles. After Denis had returned to the UK, I always seemed to be in tears and although our finances were not bad they were not good either. We had spent so much money since we had arrived in Spain and, when we examined the reasons, discovered that most of it had gone on travelling back and forth to the UK. It had also cost us a lot to find our way into the Spanish system. New roads, insurance, schooling, extra for this and extra for that—Dave had reached the stage where he had said that he wasn't going to pay out a penny more because sometimes we didn't even know what we were paying for.

I remember one time when we did get very lucky. On selling the villa, we had decided to clean out the swimming pool, a mammoth task. We released thousands of gallons of water through the pump system onto the gardens, over a slow period of time, of course. Whilst we were doing this I couldn't help but think about all the hundreds of barrels of chlorine that we had purchased to put into the pool weekly. It was wonderful having a pool but very expensive to maintain, and many, many manual working hours for Dave.

Gradually, over a few days, the pool emptied and we scrubbed the tiny mosaic-type tiles until they were sparkling. We had heard that most pools the size of ours would cost well over four hundred pounds to refill and sometimes, especially for those high up in the hills, they would have to be filled by helicopter. We had been approached by the Spanish people who owned the surrounding orange groves and Dave had made good friends with them right from the time we moved in, finding it very useful to learn his Spanish. We had grown to respect them too for their knowledge and kindness towards us. They had suggested to us that if we ever wanted, or needed, to refill the pool, then they would help us, and use the irrigation system that they used to water the groves.

It was a sight to behold, and certainly a day to remember. The pool was ready to be refilled and that afternoon three or four Spanish men turned up with all shapes and sizes of piping and tubing. Dave and I glanced at each other but said nothing. The irrigation channels ran right through our property as they did with all villas in the areas of the orange groves—one of the Spanish laws was that all workers could have access at any time, day or night. Apart from the odd worker cleaning out the gullies, we were never bothered in any way in the three years we lived there. That was one of the things that we loved about the Spanish; they never fenced anything off, they never locked up their belongings and their homes, often shabby-looking on the outside, were immaculate on the inside and so warm and welcoming. A lesson we learnt from them very quickly was that to them people were far more important than material things.

All the tubing was soon in place, small joints into large ones, some tied with string, some raised on stones over bumpy ground; one worker actually took his shirt off and wrapped it around a joint. With all this stretching approximately fifty yards, we were ready to turn on the water—well nearly ready. As with most Spanish workers a good swig of *vino blanco* (white wine) is always a good start and a good reason to celebrate, so, before the water was turned on, we all downed much more than a swig— a fair few glasses of wine. Dave and I were amazed. The water flowed through that tunnel of piping, the like of which you have never seen. Leaks sprung from every direction, which nobody was concerned about; the ground was always so dry it soon soaked away but the main flux flowed gently into the pool. The Spanish workers rushed about, chattering in their own language, giving instructions to each other whilst Dave and I watched in wonder. It took almost eight hours to fill the pool and several bottles of wine to fulfil their needs but the whole day was fantastic—laughing, joking, no bad feelings, just good honest fun. The pool was full to the top with crystal-clear pure mountain water and once again shimmering in the early evening sunlight. We offered to pay the men for their time and after refusing several times they eventually agreed to accept *dos mil pesetas* each, just ten pounds.

Selling the villa was a fairly easy decision to make; we loved its surroundings, we loved Spain and their people and we adored the climate and the carefree days, but I missed the family. Somehow there always seems to be a feeling that draws you back to the place where you feel you belong. I remember far back in my mind always feeling like this about Australia. Despite the memories of the hurt and the pain of what happened all those years ago, I still feel to this day that I am an Australian. Often when they are represented in competitions, I will find myself cheering for Australia. Dave has always made it into a joke for me and over the years I have had many presents that have related to Australia in one way or another, but right now I missed the family. Dave would say to me, 'You have all this, Susan, and still you are not satisfied,' and although I felt that Dave and I had a wonderful relationship together I couldn't help but agree with him.

We knew that selling would not be easy, having no idea of the house-selling system in Spain. We did know that there were many rules and that it could turn out to be very expensive but our minds were made up. The reasons for selling were many. The villa was old by Spanish standards, the drainage was starting to give us trouble and apparently they hadn't been emptied since time began. We had lately noticed that the covers were completely rusted over and we thought best to leave well alone. We had heard a rumour that a Dutch-owned house not far from us had heard a loud rumbling noise whilst they were in bed one evening and, on immediate inspection, they had found that their kitchen floor had erupted and risen almost four feet because of the sewer drains over-filling. We had noticed for a while that we were beginning to flush the toilets two or three times now and that was a sure sign of maintenance needed. One of the unpleasant memories of Spain was the sewer trucks constantly visiting all the villas hidden away in the hills and remote places, and the stench that always followed them.

We put up a 'for sale' sign at the entrance to the driveway and advertised in local shops and bars and also passed the word around through friends. Much to our surprise, we had several enquiries from all nationalities. I remember a German couple came, who seemed very interested and spent nearly the whole day with us, measuring and generally enthusiastic. They talked of rebuilding part of the villa, changing one thing and another, and, when they eventually left, they promised to be in touch which left us feeling full of hope and confidence. Yet we never heard from them or saw them again. Lots came just to admire our gardens. Dave and I had worked very hard on the gardens and were very proud of them.

Eventually, after many months, we had a visit from a young Spanish couple who offered us a price much below what we had originally paid for the villa. Cutting a long story short, after they had visited us on three more different occasions over a span of another three months, we relented and sold.

I remember that after we had telephoned the children to say we were coming home we visited Bill and Leila to tell them of our news. They told us they would miss us and we spent the rest of that night having one of Leila's super meals washed down with a couple of bottles of *vino blanco* and finishing with a good game of cards.

The next morning we decided to take a few weeks out and travel back to the UK. It was a long drive but we always made a mini-holiday of the journey, often reminding ourselves that we were always on one permanent holiday. We had made arrangements to stay at my sister's and telephoned the family to say we were coming. Upon arrival, everyone was pleased to see us. Many of our friends spoke of their envy of us living in Spain, and the children also missed 'all the nice bits' but, after being back for a couple of days, Dave and I soon realised that everyone was getting on with their lives. Denis was doing well at school and had made lots of new friends and seemed to be enjoying his stay with my sister. Although we knew the children loved us dearly, we felt very much like we were on the outside looking in, looking into the lives that they had carved out for themselves—I knew it was called growing up. So, when asked if they were happy that we were coming home, they said in a very nice sort of way, 'We want you to be happy and therefore do what you both think best.'

After an enjoyable stay, we drove back to Spain with a totally different outlook. I remember when we had got as far as Valencia, us looking at each other and feeling the warmth of the sun, which we loved so much, and saying, 'Let's stay.' We knew we would have the money from the villa and discussed renting somewhere and therefore we could travel back to the UK more or less every time we felt the need to see the children.

After what must have been the biggest nightmare of our lives dealing with the Spanish legal system, we sold the villa, took the money and ran. All this had taken several months, therefore we had been looking for places to live, and I, yes I again, had spotted an advert in the local English paper which read, 'mobile home for sale, three bedrooms, brand new, located on an English-run site 100 yards from beach, must be seen'.

I read it out to Dave who immediately put up his guard; whilst doing so he already knew that I had made up our minds to go and see this mobile home. One week later we saw, we purchased and we moved into our new mobile home, where we stayed for a further two years and that was a whole new 'open your eyes' experience.

CHAPTER EIGHTEEN

With a further two years now behind us, and Dave being diagnosed with a chronic lung disorder, we both agreed without hesitation to sell once again and this time to return to the UK. We had travelled many times back and forth during the past two years to visit the family and friends and I had kept up my letter-writing but we soon began to realise that there was no place like home if you are not well. It seemed that the timing was perfect as we walked away from Spain at that time without any doubts or any feelings of regret. We were both ready to go home.

The children had suggested that we could stay with them until we were able to get things sorted. They had all moved into a three-bedroomed flat together, several months prior to our returning. It was soon very obvious that the closeness of our family was very important to them and they always seemed to be there for one another and that this was made easier for them by us all living under the same roof. I remember when we turned up at their flat that they had sub-divided rooms for us to enable us to have our privacy and also for them to keep theirs. Dave and I looked for a house to buy, a reasonably priced one, as we had spent quite a bit of our money over the five years we had lived in Spain and lost on the selling of our homes out there.

Eventually we bought a house just outside of town, moved in and settled down like most people do. It was wonderful to be back with the family but like all young families they were busy getting on with their lives and we knew that this was what we had to do too. Dave's health was slowly deteriorating so I went back to work primarily to occupy myself, and, of course, the salary was also very important.

Life was very normal. We had always been a very good team, Dave and I, therefore I went out to work while he stayed home and looked after the house. I was still writing a lot of letters but now in reverse, writing to all our friends in Spain, especially Bill and Leila who had been so disappointed at our returning to the UK despite fully realising our reasons.

All the children in turn told us how pleased they were that we had returned and went on to say that although they had been praying for us to come home, they knew that it had to be our decision.

We missed the warm sunshine of Spain and the freedom that the climate gave us and the white sandy beaches and deep blue sea but were so grateful that we had had the experience of all those things despite being very happy to be home.

There were still times when my ugly past would show its face again. I remember one occasion when my youngest brother said that maybe purchasing the council house that my stepfather was residing in would be a good investment. After discussion we all agreed, and my brother went to my stepfather to put the proposal to him. He apparently agreed it would be a good idea but only for 'his' three children. He was quoted as saying, 'Not for Roy and Susan, as they aren't really family.' I remember one of my sisters being angry and saying it should be all of us or not at all. So I decided that I would go and visit my stepfather and ask him. I was forty-five years of age now and I made up my mind there and then that I would ask him outright once and for all, 'Am I family?'

I remember that day so well. Dave and I knocked on his door and he answered and invited us in with a few mumbled comments. 'What do you want then?'

He was well into his seventies now and not enjoying good health. I remember sitting down and feeling very nervous, almost feeling like a small child waiting for a good hiding. 'Make yourself a cup of tea if you want one,' he said. 'I can't manage like I used to.' I just wanted to ask my question and go—I felt so uncomfortable. Looking around the room, I saw that nothing had changed since I was a child and I could almost see my mother standing there, laying the table for tea. 'Well,' he said, bringing me back to reality with a jump, 'to what do I owe the honour of this visit?'

At first I started to stutter, then I managed to say, 'Rodney tells me that you said I am not family, so I am here to ask you outright, am I family, Dad?'

There was a long pause. Dave reached across to hold my hand and after what seemed to be forever my stepfather answered and said, 'No, you're not really, are you?'

All I remember is getting up and turning to Dave and saying, 'Come on, darling, we're leaving.' I left that house, the house that was supposed to have been my home, with a promise to myself never to return.

It was always this feeling of being unwanted that would trigger off things in my mind. After looking at some photographs one day, I came across some photos of dear Sean's wife, Flo, and her two young babies and I decided I would try and trace her and the girls. I knew that nearly thirty years had gone by and that it would not be easy to find them. I sent off a letter in reply to an advertisement in the local paper offering to help find your lost loved ones. I had to start somewhere and thought this a good place to begin. Very soon I got a reply saying they had received my application and thanking me for my information and they would do the best they could but it would take time.

That was the last I heard until nearly seven months later. Dave and I had just arrived home after a week's holiday to find a message on the answering machine: 'Sue, please ring Carol before five o'clock.' There had been several messages, all of which I related to, but not this one. 'Who is Carol?' I kept asking myself. Then, to satisfy my curiosity I dialled the number. I explained who I was and to my amazement this voice, that of Carol, said it had traced my missing family. She went on to say that she had traced my two nieces, Blanaid and Sandie, but that, sadly, Flo, their mother, who had also been my best friend, had died ten years ago. I stood frozen to the spot and tears once again filled my eyes. I cannot describe how I felt other than how sad I was that I had wasted all those years and by doing so I had missed her. I remember looking up into the sky and saying to myself, dearest Sean and Flo, you are together again.

'Hello, hello, are you still there?' said the voice on the other end of the telephone, and, holding back my tears I answered, 'Yes.' She went on to say that the two girls Blanaid and Sandie were delighted that I had traced them and would I telephone them that evening? I couldn't stop thanking her enough for her achievements and asked her how should I pay her and she said that anything I would like to donate would be extremely appreciated as all she wished to do was cover her costs. There was one other thing that I remember her mentioning and that was that whilst she was searching she had come across over six hundred people with the name of Blanaid, which really surprised me as I thought it was an unusual name. I remember all those years ago getting a letter from Flo and Sean saying they were going to call their first baby Blanaid which was Irish for Florence (Flo).

Trying my hardest to rehearse what I was going to say to Blanaid and Sandie was one of the hardest things I had had to do for a long time. I had feelings of joy for them but such sadness in my heart for their mother. I dialled the number and after leaving two nerve-racking messages on an answering machine, I managed to get through. For me, and I believe for them too, it was a wonderful moment and now we are in constant touch with each other. As soon as time permits, because of distance, we hope to be reunited, and I have promised myself, with their permission, a visit to Flo's grave where I hope I can sit for a while and make my peace.

I remember celebrating my fiftieth birthday and pausing to wonder how quickly the years had gone by and all that had gone with them. It had been twenty-five years since Denise had died and, although I loved my four children beyond words, I often would sit at her graveside and talk to her and pray that she would always be her sister's and her brothers' guardian angel.

Normal life was once again moving and although the children in turn met partners, nothing in this world could separate them from each other. They all live more or less in the same street, they all meet after work and spend their weekends out together. They all help each other out financially and, what's very special to me, they always invite Dave and me, their parents, and we spend so much time together as a family. Most of their friends will often comment on how close a family we are and many of them call me Mum so I don't feel that I have lost my family I just feel that I have gained a bigger one.

Then something strange happened. It was very near Christmas, and the doorbell rang, and the postman handed me a small package, which I signed for. I ran upstairs, tearing off the wrapping, to find that it was a book from some good friends of ours that we had met in Spain and who also had returned to the UK. They had settled in North Wales and with me still being an avid letter-writer I had always kept in touch. It was a book called *Empty Cradles* by Margaret Humphreys and just inside the front cover there was a short letter which read:

Dear Susan

Whilst in London, St Catherine's, I met a man who had been sent to Australia. Well here is the book he told me to buy for you and on page 377 is the address of the Child Migrant Trust to contact. If you get to meet the Authoress we would love to come with you. We bought ourselves a copy of the book too. It's amazing and very sad at the same time.

Love Sylvia and John

I was thrilled to bits with my present and set about reading it straightaway and I couldn't put it down. It was all about child migrants and many of the names and places triggered off memories. Whilst carefully reading every word, I began frantically to look for Roy and me in the book. The book told how hundreds and thousands of children had been sent to Australia, Canada and South Africa from England and Ireland with or without their parents' permission. It took me three days to read that book and even after I had finished it I would keep re-reading parts in case I missed something, something that would tell me the reason why my brother Roy and I were sent away. I then decided that I would write a letter to the Child Migrants Trust and in that letter I would put my case.

I did write and I enclosed a copy of a group photograph that I had, a photograph of Roy and myself aged nine and ten years, taken with a group of children just before we were put on the SS *Chitral* sailing for Australia on that fateful day, all those years ago. The photograph itself is now very crumpled and torn at the edges, but somehow I have kept this picture for most of my life and I can still name many of the other children that appear on the photograph. Attached to my letter to the Child Migrants Trust, I sent a list of the names I can still remember, never dreaming for a moment that I would get a reply. It was like a sort of therapy for me for I found that if I wrote things down, or talked about them, the better I would feel and who knows, maybe that's how books are written?

I had been out visiting my daughter and on my return home Dave had said that a man from Australia had telephoned me and would phone me back after the weekend. 'What man?' I yelled at him. I remember I seemed to get all irate. 'Didn't you take a message?' I asked. I couldn't understand why it didn't seem important to Dave—just another phone call—but to me it was feeling as if I had missed the all-important 'key' that would open the box to the story of my life.

Of course, Monday morning came as it has done since time began and I remember I couldn't settle. I kept hovering around the telephone, willing it to ring and it seemed, the more I hovered, the phone would not ring. I was soon reminded by Dave that if I kept this up I would end up a nervous wreck, so I decided to busy myself. A whole week went by and I was out visiting the family when this person telephoned again but, thankfully, this time Dave took his number and said I would call back.

The following morning, as soon as was possible, I lifted the telephone to dial this number. I remember hesitating for a while to gather my thoughts—also because I was afraid of what I might hear or that, maybe, I would hear nothing, that this was my problem and nobody else was interested or could even relate to it.

Well, is it not true that sometimes life can seem quite uncanny and that sometimes you feel that your life has been set out for you? That's how I felt when I spoke to the voice at the other end of the phone and I remember how gentle he sounded, how deeply concerned, how understanding, and his voice seemed perfect for his job. He was the person from the Child Migrants Trust who had received my letter and copy photos and I learned very quickly that over the years he had received many such letter and photographs. We spoke for over half an hour and although my case was somewhat different, as I had been returned with Roy who had been deported at that time, he said he would help me try and find some answers to all my questions. He would find out which organisation we had sailed with and make a formal request, with my permission, for my personal file.

That day, and that very moment, I felt like a ton weight had been lifted from my shoulders. I wanted to scream out loud to the whole world that at long last I was going to find out 'why'.

He had explained that there was much to do and that it would take time. He asked me to be a little patient for just a while longer and said he would be in touch as soon as he possibly could.

Within a few days I received a letter from him. The letter went through most of what we spoke of on the telephone and at the end of the letter there was an invitation for me to visit the

214

Child Migrants Office in Nottingham. He went on to say that it would be nice for us to meet and sit and talk over my anxieties with regards to my childhood as a child migrant.

I remember Dave and I quickly made plans to visit as soon as possible. I managed a few days off work and we made plans to stay over for a night in Nottingham in a hotel. Driving there, Dave and I made a few stops and enjoyed the sights. My appointment was at ten-thirty the next morning so we had plenty of time to look around and find a nearby hotel, which we did fairly easily.

Ten-fifteen the next morning, I got out of the car just outside the office and I felt as if I was going to the dentist, aware of my stomach going over. As I walked towards the door, my feet felt like two lead weights. I don't know why I felt so nervous but I do remember thinking for a second that maybe I shouldn't be bothering people with my problems, that maybe I was just making a fuss and that they would think that I was wasting their time. Still shaking, I rang the bell and a very nice lady came to the door and in a very warm and friendly voice said, 'You must be Susan.'

After all the introductions to each other were over, they made Dave comfortable in a waiting room with a cup of coffee, as he was unable to climb the steep staircase that lead to the office. The same gentleman that had telephoned me at home then sat and talked with me for well over an hour and listened carefully and understandingly to everything that I said. I remember trying to cram my whole life story into that conversation and finally he said very gently to me, 'Leave everything to me, Susan, and I will get in touch with various people and try and get hold of your personal file.' He went on to say how nice it was to meet me and how he had met several other migrants from my group who were in the photograph that I had sent, and how he would frame the photograph and place it on the wall with many others that he had received and that he would also send a copy to their Australian office. After we had said our goodbyes and he had promised to write to me as soon as there was any news, I remember walking back to the car with Dave and feeling like an over-excited child who had just received her biggest birthday present ever.

During the weeks that followed I received a phone call from my sister saying that my stepfather had been taken into hospital. I knew that he was into his early eighties and that he had been unwell for some time but I could not bring myself to visit him. I did, however, ask her, when I saw her, how he was. I remember I didn't want to feel bitter; I wasn't a person to hate, but I kept thinking of my mother dying so young and how I wished that she had lived until she was eighty and that he had died young. I kept thinking back to the beginning, back to when I was a very young child and how he had scarred me for life. I went to bed that night and struggled all night with my conscience. There was only one reason I felt that I should visit him and that was because of my younger brother and two sisters. He was their father and I was close to them, so I felt for their sakes I should be respectful. I remember he was in hospital for several weeks and still I could not bring myself to visit him. I had asked my sister to keep me informed of his condition and a few days had passed when she rang me to say that he had died. I will always remember that phone call. I don't know why but I felt so empty. I also felt angry, because I had hoped and hoped with all my heart that he would have asked for me before he died, especially as he had had the time, and maybe he might have said he was sorry—sorry for the abuse and the beatings and for sending my brother and me away, but most of all for robbing me of my mother's love. Now it was too late. I remember my sister asking me if I would like to go to the funeral and I said, 'Yes.' I don't know why I said yes. I think I was still hoping, hoping for some answers. Dave and all four of my children accompanied me to my stepfather's funeral and I remember buying some flowers and I sat all night trying to think what to write on the card. I didn't want to be a hypocrite and I didn't want to upset my youngest brother and two sisters, so I wrote a very simple message that read, 'Give my love to my mother.'

I don't know whether there is any significance but it was pouring with rain the day of his funeral. We all gathered outside his house and I noticed that Roy and his family were not there and, when I asked why, the family said that they had not been able to contact him but had left a message on his answering machine. He had moved away several years ago and none of the family including myself had seen or heard from him for a long time now. I always knew that he was still struggling to come to terms with his past and I felt sure that he would not want to be where I was right now. I also noticed that Rodney, my youngest brother, was not in the small gathering outside the house and then my sister said he was inside the house with his wife. I don't know how or what enabled me but I walked down the path and through the open front door straight into the kitchen and found Rodney sobbing and embracing his wife. I tried to comfort him and I remember feeling the most strange feeling—like I was on the outside looking in, and I could see all the small rooms that led off to another, the hallway and the stairs that led to the room I used to sleep in, and I could hear all the shouting and the arguing, and I could feel darkness all around me. I knew I couldn't stay in that house for another minute and I knew then that I never ever belonged in that house, that it only conjured up so much hate for me. And I wasn't a person to hate; I was a loving person and wanted to be a loving person, I felt so smothered.

Shortly afterwards we made our way to the church for the funeral service. I remember feeling so proud that Dave and the four children were all there with me. My stepfather, in my opinion, had never been a grandfather to my children, yet they stood there beside me to support me. After the prayers, the clergy made a speech all about what a wonderful man my stepfather had been and a wonderful husband and father. I remember looking directly at the coffin at the foot of the altar and trying, trying with all my might to feel sorry that he had died, but I could not. I felt the tears falling down my face, and my son Sean, who was beside me, gently held my hand and said to me, 'Don't worry, Mum, everything is all right now.' When the service was over, we all went to the cemetery and as I stood there with Dave and my children and watched my two sisters and younger brother crying and sobbing over the death of their father and the coffin being lowered into the same grave that my mother was buried in, my stepfather's last words to me came to mind: 'No, you're not family.'

Several weeks after the funeral I asked one of my sisters if there was anything in the house that once belonged to my mother that I could have. I was given a small brown purse, which contained two photographs and a brooch. One of the photographs was of Heidi, now Kathy, when she was first born, and the other was a small photograph of me when I was two years old, which was the age I was when my mother separated from my real father. The brooch meant nothing to me and I could not remember any connection with it and my mother but the photos were a treasure to me and to this day I am still asking myself, 'Why did my mother have these photos secretly hidden away for all those years? Did she love me?'

Remembering how Wendy and I had had such a wonderful time in Dublin last year, I decided it would be nice to go back again with all the children—Wendy and the three boys. I was working and although not wealthy, we were financially sound so I mentioned it to Dave, who agreed, but said, 'One should never go back, only forward.' He went on to say that as I had had such a good time with Wendy maybe my expectations would be too high but I decided to tempt fate and ask the children. Sean, Denis and Wendy readily agreed but unfortunately Paul was going away with his girlfriend who had booked a surprise visit to New York for him, for a Christmas present. So it was decided that just the three of them and myself would have a three-day visit to Dublin.

It was early April and our flight was leaving at seven-thirty in the morning and, although the airport was only a short distance from us, we had to be up at five-thirty to get there in time. I had made arrangements to collect each one of them as they all lived in a fairly small circle of each other. I remember waking up to a surprise heavy fall of snow and freezing cold temperature and thinking, just for a second, that maybe I should not be tempting fate after all.

Although bad weather conditions prevailed, our plane left on time and we arrived at Dublin airport to find bright, blue sky and warm sunshine. As we all piled into the taxi to take us to the hotel which, incidentally, was the exact same hotel that Wendy and I had stayed in on the previous trip, we all looked at each other, clasped hands and shouted, 'Yes.'

It was a fabulous three days and they treated me like royalty. We made a return trip to Dublin Zoo and spent the whole day there relaxing in the sunshine. As we walked up the hill towards the bus back into town I relayed the story of how their father, their Uncle Sean and Flo had walked up that very same hill with me on numerous occasions, laughing and joking, much the same as we were, almost forty years ago and once again I felt that mixed feeling of sadness and gladness. I shall always remember that short break with the children as one of continuous laughter, umpteen glasses of wine, and a warm sense of being wanted and loved.

After the plane had touched down and we had retrieved our luggage, we all thanked each other for having had such a wonderful time, remarking on how lovely the weather had been for us and here we were back in freezing England. I remember saying to Wendy, 'That's because we have Sean and Denise as our guardian angels,' and she said, 'I know.'

I had made good progress in helping the Child Migrants Trust to find out more about my childhood. I had found the children's home that was Dryleaze Home, not too far from where I live, and Dave and I eagerly went along to see it. We were informed by a very nice lady, that it is now sheltered housing accommodation for the elderly and she very kindly invited us in to look around, hoping that maybe something would trigger off my memory as much of the old building remained. Dave stayed downstairs as his breathing was exceptionally bad that day and this lady continued to show me the rest of the building. Yet nothing came to mind until she showed me a small attic room and said that it was now used as a store room. I remember feeling a cold shiver but I said nothing of this to her because I didn't want to pass on my nightmares to anyone else, certainly not to this lady, who had been so kind to me. We both thanked her and left. The next day I rang the local council for the area and after going through several departments I came across a kind voice who said she would investigate all the information I had given her regarding my brother and me being sent to Australia as child migrants from Dryleaze Children's Home and would ring me back in two or three days. I remember feeling so excited that I rang the children and they all wished me luck.

True enough, three days later, this lady rang me and said, yes, she had found my brother and me on record and that there was a whole file on us with regard to child migration. Before I could start jumping up and down for joy, she said that I would have to sign a consent form. She then went on to say that she would have to read the file to make sure there was nothing about Roy that I shouldn't know, as this was his right, and then she ended up by saying that there was a three to four month waiting list. Well, I just exploded on the phone and I asked her who gave her the right to read about me and my brother while I could not read about my own brother! I remember a choking feeling and tears welling in my eyes, and I was angry, and the voice on the other end of the telephone kept saying, 'I am sorry, Susan, that you feel this way, but you must go through the right procedure.'

I slammed the telephone down and ranted and raved around the living room. 'Who is this woman?' I shouted. 'Who does she think she is? It's my life and she still wants to control it.' I said to Dave that I was now fifty-seven years old and all this happened fifty years ago and still I didn't know why. Dave could see I was upset and did everything he could to comfort me and after I had calmed down he advised me to ring the Child Migrants Trust the next morning and let them deal with it. I did ring their office and I was advised to write to this social worker that I had spoken to on the telephone and give her instructions to deal direct with the Child Migrants Trust regarding any information that related to me. I did this and received a letter from the Trust saying that they would be in contact with me as soon as possible.

In the meantime I decided to contact Roy. It had been several years now since I had seen him, but I felt that I had enough information perhaps to attract his attention, so I rang him. His wife answered and after I had asked to speak with Roy she said that he was at work and that she would get him to ring me that evening. I waited all evening for a call but he didn't ring. I let a few more days pass and then I decided to ring again. His wife answered and she apologised for Roy not ringing me back the last time saying that he had been late getting home from work and she then asked me to hold and said she would get him for me. I don't know why but I suddenly felt flutters of excitement and then he spoke. 'Hello Susan, what can I do for you?' His voice was gentle and his caring I felt was very genuine. After an opening conversation of 'Long time no see' and 'How are you?' I went on to say that I had been in touch with the Child Migrants Trust who had very kindly offered to help me try and solve the 'mystery' of our being sent to Australia; that I had found out quite a bit of information and would like to share it with him. He replied by saying that he had decided long ago to put it all behind him and went on to say that it was lovely to hear from me again and would we, Dave and I, like to go and visit him and his wife and have a meal together? I responded with, 'Oh yes, Roy, that would be really wonderful.'

We had arranged for Dave and I to travel to them and meet at eight o'clock three days from the day we spoke on the telephone. I remember it was a warm summer evening in June and Dave and I arrived on time and Roy and his wife were there to meet us in the car park adjacent to their house. Roy was now fifty-nine years of age and I fifty-seven but, as I hugged him, I felt that we were both aged nine and ten again. I felt that something special returned that I had always felt for my brother Roy. Tears of joy welled up into my eyes along with tears of sadness, sadness of wasted years, sadness of pain and suffering that should never have been endured by two small siblings. I knew that Roy had suffered much more that me as a child and how much it had affected his life, and I knew that when he had said to me, on the telephone, that he had put it all behind him, he had done this to protect his wife and family from himself.

I had taken along some photographs, past and present, and I could see the longing and wanting in his eyes to know the answers to several questions relating to the past. His wife, much to my annoyance, but also understandably, decided very early on in the evening that we should not talk about the past. She went on to say that it would only upset Roy and that she had been through enough over the years and didn't want all the past dragged up again. At the time I was very angry but tried my hardest not to show it. We finished our meal and they walked us back to the car. His wife informed us that she would take their dog for a five-minute walk and that gave Roy and I a little time together. We hugged again, and he said that they were going on holiday and for us to give them a ring when they got back, that we would keep in touch now and not let time come between us any more. As I got into the car he leaned over and said to me, 'Why don't you give all this up, Susan? I have. It doesn't get you anywhere, all you get is a pack of lies, that's all I ever got. Nobody out there wants to tell you the truth so why bother? It's all over now.'

As I drove away and waved him out of sight, I promised myself that I would find out the truth, and when I open that 'file' I will tell my story to the world.

Two weeks after my meeting with Roy and his wife I telephoned the secretary of the Child Migrants Trust to enquire whether or not they had any news for me yet. I was informed that the kind gentleman I had previously met with was in fact on leave for six weeks and that he had not, up until he had gone, heard anything from the social services office.

I asked her to pass on my best wishes for him to have a happy holiday and put the telephone down. I felt so angry, not at the Trust but at social services. The next morning I telephoned social services and once again I put my case to them. Having already authorised them in writing to pass my file over to the Trust I explained that the gentleman dealing with my case was now away for six weeks and that I didn't want to wait another six weeks in my life so, therefore, would they please give me an appointment to visit and collect my file. Social services started to explain to me that it wasn't as easy as that, going on to say that sometimes these things took up to two years to process.

At that moment I remember screaming down the telephone at this person, 'How dare you!' and, 'Who gives you the right? I have waited long enough.' It was then that Dave, my husband, stepped in and took the telephone from me. He too then shouted down the telephone. 'Why do you insist on tormenting my wife? Who gives you the right?' he yelled at her.

I stood looking out of the window with my hands over my ears and tears rolling down my face. I felt as if I had been running for thousands of miles and had now reached my destination only to find a solid block wall in front and on all sides of me.

I turned to Dave who by now had calmed down and I listened to him pleading on my behalf.

'Next week,' I heard him say. 'Right, September 6th, Wednesday afternoon at three o'clock and, yes, she will have someone with her. Thank you very much, bye for now.'

'What did she say?' I asked, feeling a touch of excitement running through my body.

'You heard,' said Dave. 'I finally got an appointment with her for you, but you must bring someone with you'.

'Oh, I will,' I said. 'I will ask Wendy to come with me, do you think she will mind?'

'Of course she won't mind,' he said. 'Why should she?'

I couldn't contain my excitement. The day I had been waiting for was now only one week away and I knew that it was going to be the longest week of my life. I telephoned Wendy at her work place and she was so pleased for me. She promised me on the telephone that she would definitely come with me and have time off work to do so and I also made telephone calls to each one of my sons who were also very pleased, and wished me luck. After I had more or less told everyone I knew, I began to go over and over in my mind what might be in this 'file' of information that social services had been holding on me since 1949.

That night I went to bed but I couldn't sleep so I sat up in bed with a pile of old photographs in front of me and a magnifying glass. I took each photograph and examined it closely under the magnifying glass looking to see who I looked like the most. Who did I belong to? Perhaps I wasn't my mother's child, maybe that's why she didn't love me. Maybe Roy wasn't my real brother, I thought. Oh my God, I thought, what have I done? I discussed all my feelings with Dave that night, who I think by now was just glad for both our sakes to get all this out in the open and then maybe get back to our lives.

CHAPTER NINETEEN

The week that followed seemed never-ending for me and I couldn't believe that today was Wednesday 6th September 2000. Wendy arrived at two o'clock, and as the social services office was approximately fifteen miles away we left immediately to give ourselves plenty of time. Dave came with us and sat in the back of the car, being very understanding that I would want my daughter to be with me. I had discussed with him previously that maybe there would be something not very nice in the file— details of my child abuse perhaps—and, although we had no secrets, he knew I felt very strongly about this subject and would be far happier having my daughter with me.

When we arrived at the office I was shaking and although I showed excitement on the outside, inside I was so frightened. It was almost like I was a small child again and was going to the dormitory to receive a beating.

Leaving Dave in the car to read his newspaper, Wendy and I walked towards the main building. I was still shaking but she linked my arm and gave it a squeeze and said, 'Come on, Mum, you'll be all right.'

We were greeted by a young girl, who took us to a room. She said it would be nice and quiet here and offered us a cup of tea. A few minutes later the social worker, whom I had never met before but with whom I had had some very irate phone calls, introduced herself. She held a brown folder and went on to explain that she had gone against regulations and taken my file home with her the previous night to read through it to bring herself up to date as I had jumped the waiting list. She then asked me how much I knew about my past, and I told her. She also pointed out that, although I had obtained a written consent form from my brother Roy to allow me to read about him too, there were one or two letters that she could not pass on to me, namely a few medical reports together with a letter addressed to Roy personally from our mother. She said that Roy should contact her and then she would hand these letters over to him. She also said that the letter from our mother to him might be beneficial to him now in his adult years. I remember thinking, adult years! He's fifty-nine years old now. Perhaps this letter, whatever it may contain, could have saved him so much torment if he had received it years ago. I also began to wonder what was in this special letter for Roy, and why didn't I have one?

I felt very guilty standing in front of this lady who stood holding, in her grasp, the truth of my childhood. I apologised to her for my outbursts on the telephone and then introduced her to my daughter, Wendy. She handed me the file and suggested that my daughter and I read through it. She would leave the room, but in case there were any questions, she would be back later.

Inside this file were no less than forty pages of information regarding my brother and my childhood. The first was a letter from my mother dated 10th June 1949, which read:

> *Copy of original letter written by my mother and received by social services on 10th June 1949.*
> *Re: Susan age 5 yrs 6 mths and Roy age 7 yrs and 2 mths.*

> *Dear Sir*

> *I am writing to you for aid in a matter concerning two children, age five years and seven years (boy and girl). I will try to explain as well as I can. I married in 1936, then had these two*

*children. In 1947 I divorced my husband and was granted the
two children. I then married again, and now have two more
children and am expecting a third. My present husband will not
have the responsibility of my two children by my first marriage
any longer, I am receiving £1 per week allowance for them from
their father but not legally, as I did not take it to court at the
time of the divorce of which I now regret as I think I could have
got more. Anyway what I want to know is, if it's possible to have
my two eldest children put away somewhere. They are causing a
terrible lot of unhappiness between my husband and I. So I feel
sure that if they were away there would be much more happiness
all round, because they are seeing the kiddies by my second
marriage being treated with that little difference which causes
unhappiness for them. My husband will not stand the
responsibility of them any longer, and we both find under the
circumstances that we cannot do much with them. They are two
healthy children, and normal in every way, but under someone
else's training, would be much better.*

*I did hear of a case similar to mine where the government
boarded the children out, failing this, we thought of immigration
abroad. Failing everything, adoption but that is the last thing
required if it's possible for some other way. If there was any
extra expense over the present £1 of course my ex-husband
would have to pay. But I do appeal to you for help in some way
or other as I do not want my second marriage broken up. We are
exceedingly happy but for the two oldest kiddies of my first
marriage. Their father has married again and definitely wants
nothing to do with them, in fact he is the type that has no love for
children. So if you can in any way help me, I would be very
grateful.*

Yours respectfully, Mrs................

It took my daughter and I three and a half hours to read the contents of the 'file' and I have to say that having her there with me made all the difference. At long last, after all these years, it was all there in writing, how my stepfather had never wanted us, how he had abused me and put me up for adoption. How Roy had made two suicide attempts by the age of seven and how social services at that time had stated that in their opinion my stepfather had forcibly put my mother under pressure to be rid of us, and in his very own words had said, 'The further they are away the better.'

POSTSCRIPT

Just days after receiving the first proof-read for this story, my darling husband Dave was rushed into the local hospital with a chronic lung disorder. He remained critically ill in intensive care for two weeks. Then after spending a further five weeks on the respiratory ward, he came home. Still very weak, suffering from depression and connected to an oxygen machine for twenty-four hours a day, my husband's quality of life began to deteriorate rapidly. Four weeks later Dave was again rushed into hospital. The worsening of his breathing was causing carbon dioxide to build up in his body. But, with the help of a ventilating machine together with the dedication of the hospital staff, Dave once again slowly started to pull through. I was visiting Dave three times a day.

I had just arrived home from a visit one day, when I received a telephone call from one of my husband's sons. 'Sue, we have just found young David dead in his flat,' and then after a brief explanation he asked, 'Will you please tell Dad?' Young David was Dave's youngest son, aged thirty-one years. It had been well known on both sides of the family that young David had been suffering from severe depression for some time. Once again I was in the position of having to be the strong one. I couldn't scream yell or go to pieces, I knew I had to keep my self together for Dave. How would I tell him that his young son was dead, and, with himself being so seriously ill, how would he react? That evening, with the guidance and care of the doctors and nurses, I told Dave that David was dead. My darling husband Dave, died three days later.

Almost two weeks later, I attended two funerals on the same day. Among family and friends who attended I was pleased to see Roy and my younger brother and two sisters. That day, crying and bewildered, I stood at the front of the chapel with my children, Paul, Sean, Wendy and Denis at my side. For a moment my thoughts returned to my mother, my baby daughter Denise, dearest Ma and young Sean and my best friend Flo. And now young David and his father, my husband, who was the love of my life, and whose patience and understanding and love for me and my children was like no other. With tears rolling down my face I looked up towards the altar and asked God one more time, Why?

Working full-time looking after the elderly and having acquired two small puppies to keep me company, I am coping with my changed life. My love for my children keeps me strong. Therefore, I can't help thinking that perhaps the same could have worked for my mother.